amazon.co.uk Reviews...

⭐⭐⭐⭐⭐ **Brilliant! It works.**

By Amanda Cahun on 21 August 2016

Verified Purchase

I got this for my Son in January to prepare for A2 exams in the summer. It wasn't a magic wand but what it did was give him confidence, made him focus and plan, and provided revision techniques which I believe definately work! Very easy reading and inspiring. My Son needed high grades but had been disappointed with his AS grades of ABC. He has just achieved AAB and is off to study Veterinary Medicine. Of course he put in the hard work but this book definately gave him the focus and realisation of what is needed to get high grades. Definately worth a try, you've got nothing to loose!

⭐⭐⭐⭐⭐ **My AS grades weren't brilliant, but a year later**

By Amazon Customer on 18 August 2016

Verified Purchase

When I bought this last year, I was a bit skeptical but a year later I can say that without it I would not have improved so greatly. My AS grades weren't brilliant, but a year later, after following the advice in the book, I did much better than the previous year. This is a great book, as long as you follow the steps!

D1465260

3

⭐⭐⭐⭐⭐ **This book will change your life.**

By Amazon Customer on 26 August 2016

I remember after receiving my AS results last year, I was very disappointed in myself as I walked away with ADE. After purchasing this book I've read it three times since. I had everything to lose...my uni place and my future career. This book honestly made me realise its all about your mindset and how hard you work. I then decided to changed my business a level to btec , in which meant I had to do two years worth of work in one. And also I had to move my E grade at sociology to a B, I had to retake every single one of my exams. This book isn't just about teaching you how revise, it teaches you how to stick to your goal in life. And how to achieve your goals and ever since I've stuck with a positive mindset. I followed the book step by step, every time I felt like giving up I kept looking at my post it note I made when I first read the book, in which had my dream uni, my course and grades I wanted to achieve. In which was Distinction, A, B. I knew if I achieved these grades I'd be proud. I collected my results last week and I achieved distinction *, A, A. I moved from an E at AS to an A at A2. Thanks to this book, it helped me change my whole mindset to my goals in life and also taught me how to revise. I definitely recommend this book to everyone taking their A levels, this book teaches you so much that your school won't.

 **Buy it!**

By Amazon Customer on 17 February 2017

I received ABC on my AS results and have been offered a place at my first choice university thanks to this book. I had absolutely no idea how to revise until this book and it is true, looking through your folder a few times isn't revision, but this gives you options and a complete motivation changer. The best thing is that I still had free time and I wasn't doing 10 hours straight like GCSEs, it means my revision is much better and I'm far more rested. Seriously buy it! It's worth the money and even if you don't agree with the methods, the confidence booster is definitely priceless

Amazing revision technique which helped me achieve great A2 results

By Claire on 14 August 2015

Verified Purchase

I bought this book back in March time before sitting my A2 exams. After rather disappointing AS results I was very thankful to discover this. I went from getting a U in one of my exams to an A after taking the exam again, all that changed was my revision technique. Amazing revision technique which helped me achieve great A2 results!

★★★★★ DEFINITELY READ THIS BOOK!

By Katie on 19 August 2015

Verified Purchase

Amazing. I will definitely be putting this into practice as I feel I am in a very similar situation to the author currently. I work hard but nothing really shows for it and admittedly I don't cope in exam conditions, however I feel as though this book has lifted the fog on things find I actually do but shouldn't as it is hindering my potential. I recommend this book if you are looking for a new leaf for a new year be it A-level, or GCSE, or even parts in reference to just everyday life. This is just a book that everyone should read at least once at one point in their lives. I have recommended this book to my own family to read, as I feel that they will be able to understand the position I feel I am now in as a result of my actions and in a way how they may be able to support me in how I progress over the next year. DEFINITELY READ THIS BOOK!

★★★★★ Definately recommend to EVERY A level student

By Amazon Customer on 11 March 2016

Verified Purchase

Amazing! Really useful for the students who like me we're in a 'rut', so stressed with my looming AS level exams! This book simply outlines what your doing that wrong and how little changes can make a big impact! Definitely helped me plan my revision and have a better understanding on how useful my revision techniques actually are.

For more reviews, please visit www.amazon.co.uk or www.AcademicUnderdogs.com

4

HOW TO
ACE
YOUR A-LEVELS

**Inspired by Student Success Stories.
We Tell You What Your Teachers Don't.**

A . R A J A
M . K A R I A

Published by Anshul Raja
Academic Underdogs

Printed in the United Kingdom

Cover design by Zahid Pirani

First Printing, 2015

ISBN 978-0-9933488-0-8

How to ACE Your A-Levels
Roberts House, 2 Manor Rd, Ruislip, Middlesex HA4 7LB

www.AcademicUnderdogs.com

To my family

Contents

First things first...

The three step plan...

Onwards & upwards...

Introduction

You know those skinny Indian kids who look like they are too young to have a moustache? That was me in high school and unsurprisingly I didn't sit too high up on the social food chain. This would have been ok if I was a top student because I'd only have to endure a few awkward years in high school. Then I could have a future filled with a great career, money and women. Unfortunately, I wasn't good at exams either!

After waving goodbye to high school with pretty mediocre GCSEs, I started my AS levels at a new school with a new found determination. Achieving good grades and getting into university meant everything to me. So I made a real effort throughout the year. Unfortunately, this wasn't enough. Despite working hard and listening to my teachers, on AS level results day, I ended up with Ds and Us – Brilliant!

I joke about it now but those grades really hurt. After results day I went straight home, ran up to my room, sat on my bed, looked at the floor and whispered to myself... "What is wrong with me? Why am I so rubbish? I'm clearly not intelligent enough. It must be my genetics. Look at my Biology grade – do I even know what genetics means?!!"

To make matters worse, 70% of the grades achieved at my school were B or above and all of my friends did really well. Even the front pages of all the newspapers showed a nationwide improvement. People kept asking me how my exams went and I felt so embarrassed about telling them. Others gave me sympathy and advice when I didn't even ask for it. I knew they meant well but all it did was make me feel even worse!

What now?

There were a bunch of questions running through my head at the time. Should I give up and do a vocational course? Or get a job somewhere and work my way up? My teachers, some friends and even my own family were subtly encouraging me to consider these options too. It just didn't feel right. I had to give it one more go.

My entire life I had held this belief that no matter how hard I tried, I just wasn't capable at succeeding. Not only at school, but also everything else. Sports, music, art and pretty much everything I tried. Maybe I wasn't as good as these A and A* students around me but I would never know for sure unless I really tried this time. For the first time, it didn't become about getting into university or my future career, just about proving it to myself. If I put all my energy and efforts into preparing for exams, and still didn't achieve the grades I wanted then fair enough. Fine, then I'd lower my expectations and stop dreaming about becoming a doctor or successful businessman. However, if I did succeed, then I'd know for a fact that I was the issue and not my capabilities. I needed to find out for myself and that is what motivated me to retake almost all my first year exams in year 13 alongside all the rest of my exams.

The game plan

Over the next few weeks, I researched everything I could about studying and exams. From reading books about memory retention to speaking with successful and experienced students. From this I produced a set of goals and a written game plan.

Goals and plans were nothing new to me. I'd made plenty before without acting on them, but this time it was different. I believed in my plan and, as I started preparing for the next set of exams, I could see evidence that it was working. The sting of my previous results combined with the early signs of progress created momentum that stayed with me the entire year. By study leave the

12

following year, I had executed my strategy and walked into most of my exams with much more confidence.

This time on results day I left with straight As with many module marks exceeding 90%. It was one of the biggest turn arounds some of my teachers had ever seen. My parents and friends were completely shocked!

At university, I used the same principles and techniques again, and it worked. I left UCL with a first-class honours in chemical engineering. My results were in the top 5 percent of the year and I was awarded with a certificate of academic excellence by the Dean of students.

How to ACE Your A-Levels

Ever since completing my A-Levels countless students approached me for help. It started with friends and family, but as word spread, random people began contacting me for guidance. Everyone who used my approach improved their grades and future prospects.

As demand increased, it became obvious that schools were falling short when it came to study skills and motivating their students. Eventually I decided to gather all the golden nuggets I had built up over the years and put them into one resource. How to ACE Your A-Levels was born!

Since publishing this book, it has been a consistent Amazon #1 best seller year on year and has sold thousands of copies. We have been inundated with messages from students across the globe thanking us for our help. It only takes a glance at our reviews on Amazon, testimonials on Facebook or comments on YouTube to realise how effective this approach is.

What's in the book?

On the surface, How to ACE Your A-Levels is a strategy book that will show you how to achieve As and A*s in your exams. My 3-step plan will describe how to:

1. Plan your revision from now until exams
2. Use learning techniques that work
3. Choose the correct resources to learn from
4. Tailor your study technique to the subjects you are taking
5. Improve your daily routine and habits
6. Maintain your motivation right up till exams

Beneath the surface, this book is about how to bounce back from disappointment and create a winning attitude. Till this day, whenever I find myself in a deep hole (I've been in a fair few!), I still think back to my A-Levels. This is because it was the first time I took matters into my own hands, backed my ability and won. The experience left me with a tenacious personality and a pit-bull type resilience that I wouldn't trade for any amount of intelligence.

That's the real reason why all the late nights, hours of work and pressure of exams are worth it. Getting good grades, into a top university and securing a dream career are by-product of a winning mind set. This is what I hope you achieve after finishing this book!

My goal is to not only show you the door, but also inform and inspire you to a point that it's almost impossible not to walk through it and achieve your dreams.

Thank you for reading How to ACE Your A-Levels and trusting my guidance!

First thing's first...

1 What's the point?

The first and most important step in getting your desired A-Levels is to understand why you need good A-Level grades...

While I was in school, I couldn't help but think the following:

-   "I'm only going to be young once, so why should I waste it reading book after book?"

-   "Are A-Levels really a critical point in my life? It seems like everything is 'critical'; 11+ exams, SATS, GCSE's."

These are by far, the most obvious and frustrating questions which go through the minds of most students, and worst part is that no-one can give us an honest answer!

However, the honest truth is that: A-Levels really do matter.

Why are A-Levels important?

Being successful in your A-Levels will open you up to a world of freedom and respect from a number of individuals. This includes your parents, family, teachers and friends.

Having good A-Levels is like a passport: it will allow you to go to a university, enrol into something which you want to do and will open up many job opportunities. In fact these days many top companies screen candidates by setting a minimum requirement for UCAS points before offering interviews.

School teaches you a lot, but sometimes teachers have a hard time convincing students that A-Levels are important. Without knowing why you want to do well, it will be hard motivate yourself enough to study hard and make a sacrifice. Some people don't even realise that sacrifices need to be made.

One thing is for sure, in order to achieve high grades, you will need to make a few sacrifices.

Can you make the sacrifice?

When I was a student, all I wanted to do was chase girls and play Call of Duty (COD). I couldn't care less about the differentiation of X^2. I still don't. But, you have to understand that sacrificing these things is essential for success.

The way I look at it, is that in the grand scheme of things, missing out on a couple of hours on COD is not going to kill you. Some people will say it's not a sacrifice, because you can make revision fun. Certainly, you can make it interesting. But at the end of the day, no matter how many picture diagrams or YouTube videos you use to make revising more interesting, you'd probably prefer playing a game or going to the pub with your mates.

BUT, just tell yourself, sacrificing some time during a few school terms in your life is absolutely worth it for the following core reason:

Ace Tips

Achieving good grades at A level will give you a better chance of getting into a better university which will give you a better chance of landing a higher paying job which will give you a better chance of living a richer/lavish lifestyle.

Plain and simple.

Imagine yourself in 2 year's time

Right now, most of you live at home with your family. You have to be home at a certain time. You can't make too much noise. Your parents are always nagging you.

If you get your desired grades, you are in control of your life.

Within two years, you will have your own accommodation as far away from home as you wish. You will have your own curfew, wake up with a whole new set of friends. You will have the most freedom you can possibly imagine at a young age, in a city of your choice, studying a course of your choice, allowing you to recreate your own identity.

There will be plenty of facilities available for you to achieve your potential in whatever way you choose, whether that be Muay Thai boxing, becoming a poker player or writing journal articles for the university magazine.

These few years will most definitely be the most exciting years of your life. Take me for example, I chose to go to university in London for the sole reason of being able to live in the most buzzing city in the UK. In the first three months, I was out partying every night, only to wake up to go to lectures I was actually interested in and I wanted to go to. You don't want to be in a small university which no-one has ever heard of, with a tiny student union and sports pitch, doing a 'Mickey Mouse course'.

Investing and sacrificing time during your A-Levels will not only provide you with a passport to gain all of this for the next three or four years, but also the excellent career opportunities a UK university degree can offer you.

"It will be fun, but with graduates having fewer job opportunities these days, is there any point in going to university?"

Universities currently ask for £9,000 per year (this is set to increase), which you have to pay back incrementally once you graduate and start earning over a certain amount. This means you will be in debt of at least £27,000 as you leave university.

This is quite a difficult decision, particularly when there is no guarantee you will leave with a graduate job. However, your prospects of securing a graduate job are higher if you have high A-Level grades, and if you study at a top university.

If you can secure a university admission in a Redbrick University, potential employees will look at you more favourably.

Going to university is, like anything else, an investment. An investment of time and money. High A-Level grades provide you with a better university and course, and therefore better returns on your investment.

In summary: what do you have to do?

1. Accept that you will have to make a sacrifice to achieve good A-Level grades. There is no way around it.

2. Identify what university you want to go to, what course you want to do and why. Imagine:
    *   Where do you would want to live?
    *   Who do you want to live with?
    *   What type of friends do you want?
    *   Do you want to go to a city centre full of clubs, or spend time at the seaside in?
    *   Would you rather study abroad?

Browse through the university prospectuses and university websites to help with this. Doing all this early in the year will not only help you prepare, but also get you motivated.

3.   Write all this down and stick it somewhere in your room so you have something to visually remember.

2 The 3 stooges

Do you ever feel that there is a missing piece somewhere, or a screw lose in your brain that doesn't let you become the person you want to be? I used to feel like that all the time. I thought there was something inherently wrong with me that stopped me from succeeding in exams. I believed that those who did well had some special X-factor that I lacked. I also thought that these problems were permanent. There were 3 main thoughts that kept coming into my head:

1. I'm not smart enough
2. My school is rubbish
3. I didn't do well at GCSEs, how can I do well now?

Sound familiar? I called these the 3 stooges. Whenever I couldn't understand something in my textbook, or got stuck on a hard question, these thoughts would appear. More often than not, I would then get up from my desk and start procrastinating. Watching TV or playing games became a coping mechanism or a way to distract me from feeling insecure. In other words, I was running away from my insecurities instead of facing these head on.

In hindsight this was false. I was smart enough and my school wasn't the issue but, I had recycled these thoughts so many times that they became facts. It's only when I questioned these insecurities, did I then start controlling them and stop them from controlling me.

Pointing fingers at my intelligence or school also showed that I had a **Fixed Mindset**. An individual with a fixed mindset believes that their abilities are constant and will never change. A **Growth Mindset**, on the other hand, is when you believe your abilities are a variable that can improve with effort or by making the right choices.

What mindset do you have?

You probably have an idea already, but if you aren't sure, just keep an eye on your thoughts particularly while working. Usually when you are alone at home doing some homework or preparing for a test your true beliefs will surface. Write them down and just take a moment to reflect. Are they similar to these?

Fixed mindset

1. I don't have enough time
2. I can't concentrate for long periods
3. I'm just not good at this subject
4. I have no genuine interest in this stuff

Or these?

Growth mindset

1. I can do this if I just work a little harder
2. I need to be more organised
3. I have to stop dwelling over the past – it doesn't help
4. I need to be more resilient

If I asked you to rate your mindset from 1 to 10, 1 being a completely fixed mindset and 10 being a growth mindset, what number would you give? Of course, to improve your chance at succeeding in exams or anything else, you want to be close to a 10.

Why is a growth mindset important?

It stops you from lowering your standards after a recent set back or failure. When mentoring students who have underachieved in their exams, I breathe a sigh of relief when they are hysterically upset at themselves for not doing their best. Not because I like to see someone in pain, but as this is usually a sign of a growth mindset. Being in distress, shows that they haven't given up on themselves (even if they say they have). It also shows that they know there is a way to reach their goals, but haven't figured out how yet.

How to develop a growth mindset

Developing the right mindset requires challenging and potentially altering your beliefs. This is easier said than done! Beliefs are stubborn because they form over long periods of time. Also, you can't really choose to believe something or not. Either the evidence for or against that belief satisfies you or it doesn't.

To build a growth mindset, you need to actively seek out the evidence and become a bit of a sceptic. This is exactly what I did and what I recommend you do too. To help, the next chapters will discuss the 3 most common assumptions or beliefs that tend to hold people back from succeeding in exams.

2a <u>I'm not smart enough</u>

Students think about intelligence far too much and I was no exception. Whenever I got stuck on practice questions or struggled to understand something, I always used the excuse: "I'm not smart enough".

The first lesson of this chapter is important.

<u>**Getting high grades at A-Levels is not all about intelligence**</u>

When it comes to intelligence, A-Level students can be split into those with average intelligence and those with high intelligence. They can also be placed into good and bad work technique categories.

Each student in any given academic year group can therefore be separated into the following 4 categories:

Average Intelligence + Bad Work Technique	High Intelligence + Bad Work Technique	Average Intelligence + Good Work Technique	High Intelligence + Good Work Technique

Remember, no-one doing A-Levels is of low intelligence. This is because colleges require you to have a certain number of GCSE's in the A*- C or 9 - 4 boundary to be accepted to sit A-Levels. This system is designed to avoid wastage of government resources on people who are deemed to be incapable of managing their academic work. **Therefore, if you are accepted on an A-Level course, you have enough intelligence to complete your A-Levels.**

Our research has shown us:

The grades you get will depend on your work technique, not on your intelligence.

If you have never performed well academically, through school and GCSE's, you probably fall into the category of average intelligence and bad work technique. In addition, if you feel like you're doing enough work, but still not obtaining the grade you want, make no mistake it's highly unlikely that it is because of your intelligence; you are simply not doing enough, or not studying properly.

You may feel anger to what I have just said. Who am I to say that your inability to do well at exams has nothing to do with your intelligence? If you feel that it is your intelligence that is holding you back, I am a living, breathing example of why that is not the case.

I have never been able to grasp concepts easily or memorise something by reading it once. I completely failed my AS levels, but when it came to my final year, I left with straight A's. Did my natural intelligence suddenly increase in one year or was it really that my intelligence played a small part in achieving my desired grades?

I, like many, used to get frustrated that there seemed to be lots of 'naturally' intelligent people among my peers. Some of my friends seemed to just 'get it', understanding and absorbing information with much less effort than what I put in. I used to think that I would not be able to achieve the same grades as them. But in my final year, I had an epiphany and came to realise that just because they didn't need to spend as much time and effort understanding, didn't mean that I wouldn't succeed. It just meant I'd need to sacrifice a bit more of my time.

Cursing your intelligence is pointless because it is a constant you are born with and cannot change.

> "The measure of our future success and happiness will not be the quality of the cards we are dealt by unseen hands, but the poise and wisdom with which we play them. Choose to play each hand to the best of your ability without wasting the time or energy it takes to complain about either the cards or the dealer or the often unfair rules of the game. Play both the winning and the losing hands as best you can, then fold the cards and ante up for the next deal!"
>
> -- Joe Klock

Natural intelligence is not one required to get high A-Level grades. Smart studying is the secret. This further explains the reason why top schools repeatedly get 99% of students achieving top grades. These schools aren't filled with geniuses.

A-Levels test your **1) dedication and 2) ability to meet deadlines.** These two qualities are absolutely essential to do well at university, and are also important during A-Levels.

A-Levels are easier than university

It always irritated me when people said A-Levels are really easy compared to university. However, after leaving university, I realised that they were right. Right now you have access to a lot of resources. These include structured learning outcomes, past exam questions, core textbooks, all of which help you to maximise marks. At university, there are no revision aids or concise learning outcomes on hand to help.

For example, let's compare an A-Level learning outcome to a university one. For biology A-Level, the learning outcomes would ask you to "define homeostasis", while a university guideline would be "gain an understanding of the mechanisms of homeostasis." University learning outcomes are much broader and they require extra reading just to achieve 60% (a C). For A-Levels, if you had learnt the recommended examining board book off by heart, you'd be well on your way to achieving an A or an A*, as most of the marks you need can be obtained with knowledge of the recommended book.

A-Levels test your ability to learn a given amount of information in a small period of time. They provide you with all the information; then use exams to test your dedication to the course material and use coursework to test your ability to meet deadlines.

To summarise...

When people adopt a fixed mindset and blame external influences, they completely disregard a huge list of other factors which help them do well at A-Levels. Such as:

- The method by which you revise
- Time management
- Procrastination and how to avoid it
- Motivation
- Revision environment
- Which subjects to study first
- When to start revising
- When to stop revising
- What to do the day before the exam

By dismissing your chances and saying "I am not smart enough so I will not pass", you have not even attempted to consider how any of these factors come in to play. This book will ensure that all the above factors are dealt with so you will get the grades you want. However, before we can tackle these areas, you must accept that intelligence is not holding you back, as, believe me, when it comes to A-Levels, intelligence really doesn't matter.

2b My school is rubbish

Why do you think that the same schools appear on the top of the league table each year, without fail?

These top schools work by providing two tools:

1) A solid working environment with reward for hard work
2) Repetition: reinforcement of learning

The environment

In these top schools, 99% of pupils are not more intelligent then you. They have the same cohort of students as are at yours. Yet, 99% get good A-Levels, repeatedly, year after year.

These students have the same information as you. They have access to the same module aims and books. The difference is their school environment.

The environment means that people strive to do better than others. It is accepted that work is important among students. Students don't attend lessons trying to play games and laugh at someone locking the teacher out of the room. They attend because they want to excel above their peers. The superficial concept of studying not being 'cool' doesn't exist. The environment creates competition and an innate desire for success, bringing about motivation within its students.

You probably didn't choose the school you are currently enrolled in. Also, in most circumstances, you cannot change the school you are in. They are the cards you have been dealt with.

There is no doubt that having a good working environment is key to achieving strong A-Levels and the 'study cycle' chapter will cover this.

Why spend time learning how to make a cake, if you're not going to bake it?

Reasons for failure often given by students include: the lessons are poor, the teachers can't speak English, no-one pays attention or there is too much noise.

Essentially, unlike younger years in school, the structure of a lesson at A-Level is more like that of a university lecture. Classroom time is there simply to introduce the material and to answer any obvious questions students may have in that short space of time.

The other main purpose of a lesson is to help structure your learning so that you complete all your homework, mock exams and learning outcomes before the exam.

By introducing the topic, completing homework and mock exams you cover the same information three or more times. With further personal revision, students can walk into the exam having covered the same information up to 6 times! This is where the top schools *really* stand out.

Take for example a chapter from Shakespeare's Hamlet:

A school with a 99% A-Level pass rate asked students to read Act 1-2 before the lesson. From there the Act 1-2 would be discussed in the lesson. Homework would be set to encourage further reading.

Students would have to revise for mock exams, complete the mock exam and correct it. Through this process, the student will have learnt about Hamlet up to 6 times.

The quality of the actual teaching provided within that half an hour is of limited importance. What is of more importance is the total number of times that a subject has been reinforced and re-discussed, because it improves the chance of remembering information in the exam.

Top schools make this easier for students as they encourage them through homework, pre-reading and mock examinations. Therefore, if the lesson itself is of a poor standard and you feel that you are not learning anything, relax. That does not mean that you will fail your exams. Chances are, no matter how poorly the lesson is taught, there will be tools to ensure that learning material is re-covered again and again.

You cannot control how good or informative your lessons are, they are entirely out of your control. What really makes a difference is what you do outside of the classroom. I will discuss this further within the three step programme.

2c I didn't do well at

GCSEs

My GCSE grades were pretty average and I often felt down about them, particularly when I spoke to others who never seemed to have anything less than A or A* grades! This, combined with all the positive success stories splattered across newspapers, gave me the false impression that everyone was a genius apart from me and that I didn't stand a chance against them. I thought universities would take one look at my GCSE grades and click 'next' on UCAS. This belief killed my motivation and kept knocking me back. Oh, how wrong I was!

While strong GCSE grades can put you in good stead for university applications and future career prospects, it's not too late to make change. If you achieve high grades at A-Levels, your GCSE's matter a lot less. Have a look at the university prospectuses. By far, the majority of courses ask for good A-Levels and a very minimum number of GCSE's. Remember, they are assessing interest in the subject, dedication and ability to meet deadlines!

If you meet the grade requirements for each of your desired courses, university admissions will accept that you have the basic academic abilities to proceed with the course. More emphasis is then placed on other personal qualities, which are highlighted in your reference and personal statement. GCSE grades only play a very small part. Therefore if you have not done well at GCSE's, do not let this define you. The people reading your UCAS forms are human, they too remember what it was like to be 15.

Many point to their GCSEs and say 'look that's proof I don't have what it takes'. Then at university they will point to both their GCSEs and A-levels and say the same thing. This can carry on far far into adulthood if you let it. I've met people ten years older than me who look at their salary over the past few years and use that as a way to measure their self-worth. At some point, you have to break the cycle. Now is the perfect time to do it! And If you do, the next time you feel that you can't do something (or if someone tells you), you will stop and think 'hold on a second – look at my A-levels. Look how much I improved. I'm going to keep trying'.

The harsh truth

Having read this chapter, you should now know that:

1. You have to make a sacrifice to get your desired A-Level grades and there is no way around it
2. Sacrifice is worth it due to the potential huge rewards
3. You are smart enough to get your desired A-Level grades and saying that you are not is merely an excuse and an instant set-up for failure.
4. You, and solely you, will be to blame for failing your A-Levels; not your teachers, school, 'natural intelligence', parents or anything else.

You must be willing to accept that your number one goal is to achieve your desired grades. In doing so, you will be able to accomplish the personal rewards which you identified in Chapter 1, and go to the university of your choice.

The three step plan...

3 <u>How to achieve your</u> <u>desired grades</u>

On AS results day, I got my results (DDDU), and made a conscious decision to change. I used my bitterness and anger to drive me, and as a result this anger gradually turned into productive thoughts. I grabbed a pen and started brainstorming a plan. Somehow the little voice in my head constantly telling me to do it later became very quiet.

It was at this point I realised that two types of people existed. Those who were pro-active and would revise throughout the year and then those like me, who would wait until they had to revise.

<u>Pro-active vs. reactive</u>

I would wait until the very last moment, when an exam or coursework deadline was looming and this would be what I used for motivation to study. I realised that this wasn't just about exams: it was every part of my life. I wouldn't clean my room until my parents threatened me with no dinner. I wouldn't install anti-virus software on my computer until my computer stopped working. I would leave my ironing until the morning before school. I wouldn't shave for an entire week until I had a biology class, because I knew that my biology teacher (ex-army) would make me clean up litter for the entire lunch time if I wasn't clean shaven. There used to be a bus that came to school every day to pick us up from a road ten minutes walking distance from my house at exactly 7.40 every day. I would wake up at 7.20 only because I had to, otherwise I would have to walk an extra 20-30 minutes to catch a train and then walk up an enormous hill. I am ashamed to say that I missed that bus at least once a week, just because I wanted those extra minutes in bed, and I knew that I didn't technically have to wake up: after all, I could still get to school by train!

Looking back, I cringe at how completely 'reactive' I was. My motivation to be productive solely depended on certain situations and circumstances which forced me to be productive. If there was no pressure, I would get nothing done.

The benefits of being a pro-active person

After failing my AS levels, I decided to get rid of my reactive ways and attempted to be pro-active. Instead of ignoring and pushing looming deadlines to the back of my mind, I would face them head first. Rather than waiting around for the inevitable deadlines of exams and coursework, I would plan for these. I would iron my clothes and shave the evening before, and wake up those few minutes earlier. Having been both a reactive and proactive person, I can honestly say that being pro-active is so much less stressful: you are not constantly rushing, worried and pressured to meet the next deadline. Instead, you are working at a relaxing and manageable pace.

Second year was still challenging, but I had time to enjoy other activities, such as meeting friends, cycling, swimming and going on dates. This was much more enjoyable as I didn't feel guilty or fear upcoming deadlines and exams, as I had already planned for them as opposed to cowardly ignoring their existence as I did before.

It was this realisation and change in my mindset that allowed me to create a pro-active plan to get top grades at A-Level. This plan forced me to face deadlines. It consisted of simple strategies in each of my subjects to prepare myself, so that I learned almost everything I needed for the next set of exams.

38

I started from scratch, pretending it was the start of my AS levels, and took no shortcuts in spite of obvious time constraints. At this point, I knew that I wanted top grades at A-Levels and I knew why. I wanted to go to a top university and study a top degree. I just didn't know how to.

The pro-active plan

In the pro-active plan, there are three main steps that any student must go through before they take their exams:

1. **Method (chapter 4):** Top students tend to keep their cards close to their chest, never giving much away. This section reveals all by introducing the most effective and efficient techniques for learning information. I also show you what to revise and how to plan revision from now till exam day.

2. **Study cycle (chapter 5):** What exactly is hard work? Every-one tells you to do it but no-one really explains what it is or how to do it. I believe hard work is a skill in itself and has to be practised. In this section, I'll give you all the tools to help you gauge how much is enough.

3. **Motivation (chapter 6):** This section is the 'fuel' for the study cycle. Here I show you how to push yourself to study each day, so that you have the energy and enthusiasm to work through the study cycle.

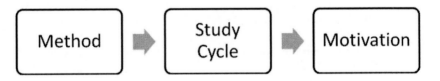

4 Step 1 – Method: what the A graders don't tell you

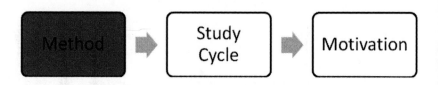

This chapter is all about the no-nonsense practical advice made by students for students. I've interviewed a number of successful A-Level graduates and put their views together. Some of the content is controversial, and your teachers may not agree with my concepts. However, these are the methods which have worked for me, many others and which will work for you.

This chapter will be explained using a top-down approach starting with revision planning and then moving on to effective learning techniques.

The layered learning timetable

The dangerous assumption

The most common and detrimental assumption made by students is this...
"I'm not going to start revising now because I'll forget everything before the exam anyway".

It is important to realise that if you resort to last minute cramming then you will not retain enough information to achieve a high mark. For the volume of information you need to learn for A-Levels, you will need to use <u>repetition</u> or layered learning. This is the key to achieving high marks in these and future exams.

Repetition theory

About a year ago, I went to visit some of my family for dinner. Climbing up a dusty staircase, I found my hunched over younger cousin, James, frantically hunting through a revision guide. He looked stressed, so I asked him what's wrong.

James: "I've got 2 months till my exam, I've just started revising and I don't know anything!"

Me: "How many subjects have you got?"

James: "Four - Chemistry, Biology, History, Physics"

Me: "Ok, so how have you planned your revision?"

James: "Well, I have 8 weeks left and 4 subjects. So I'm going to spend the first 2 weeks revising Chemistry, two weeks revising Biology, two weeks revising History, and two weeks revising Physics."

Me: "OK, and how will you revise Chemistry in the first two weeks."

James: "I'll run through the entire subject, from start to finish."

At this point I told him the brutal truth: he was NOT going to do well.

He looked shocked, as do many people when I bluntly reveal this. After all, what was he doing wrong? He's still got two months, he's revising systematically through all the subjects.

James is a hard worker and while I knew he would spend two months locked up in his room revising, his revision timetable had two major faults:

1) He only covers each subject once.
2) By the time the exams arrive, he would have forgotten the first subject he revised.

The standard revision timetable (James's revision timetable)

No. of days before exams: 80 **Number of subjects: 4**

No. of days before Exam	Plan
Day 80-60	Revise Subject 1: Start to finish
Day 60-40	Revise Subject 2: Start to finish
Day 40-20	Revise Subject 3: Start to finish
Day 20-0	Revise Subject 4: Start to finish

Subject	No. of Repetitions
Subject 1	1
Subject 2	1
Subject 3	1
Subject 4	1

The standard revision timetable is not the best way to revise for exams. A good revision timetable must incorporate layers. To do well in your exams, you must go through the same subject material **at least three times.**

I tried to explain this to James:

Me: "James, your 'standard' revision timetable means that you will only have gone through each subject once and you will have forgotten it all when you get to the exam! You have to go through all the subjects at least three times otherwise you will fail!"

James: "That's impossible, keep dreaming. I only have 80 days and have four subjects to revise before my exams. How on earth do you expect me to go through everything three times? "

Me: "I have a method you can use in the same amount of time which I can guarantee that you will get the grades you want."

It was at this point that I told James about the revision timetable I had used throughout all my examinations and which has not once failed me, layered learning...

What is layered learning?

Layered learning involves revisiting the same information again and again. The basic idea is that the more times you cover a piece of information the longer it stays in your memory. Therefore, the higher the chance you have of remembering the content during the exam. It also revolves around the basic principle of the more you repeat the slower you forget. This is shown in the diagram below.

Repetition Graph

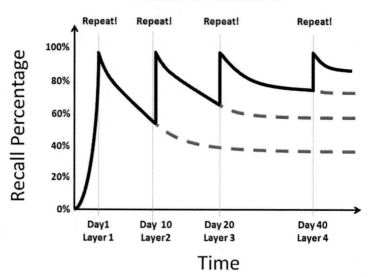

In Chapter 3, we identified that the majority of students in top schools consistently achieve top marks. This is not because they have smarter students, but simply due to maximising the re-enforcement of learning and encouraging you to go over the same information again and again. This ensures that it is retained.

The layered learning revision timetable (My revision plan)

No of days before exams: 80
Number of subjects: 4

No. of days before Exam	Plan	
Day 80-70	Revise Subject 1: 1st thorough repetition	Layer 1
Day 70-60	Revise Subject 2: 1st thorough repetition	
Day 60-40	Revise Subject 3: 1st thorough repetition	Total 40 days
Day 40-30	Revise Subject 4: 1st thorough Repetition	
Day 30-25	Revise Subject 1: Moderate repetition	Layer 2
Day 25-20	Revise Subject 2: Moderate repetition	
Day 20-15	Revise Subject 3: Moderate repetition	Total 20 days
Day 15-10	Revise Subject 4: Moderate repetition	
Day 10-8	Revise Subject 1: brief repetition	Layer 3
Day 8-6	Revise Subject 2: brief repetition	
Day 6-4	Revise Subject 3: brief Repetition	Total 8 days
Day 4-2	Revise Subject 4: brief repetition	
Day 2-0	Skim through material and Rest	Recap Two days

Subject	No. of repetitions
Subject 1	3
Subject 2	3
Subject 3	3
Subject 4	3

The 'layered learning revision timetable' is completed in the same amount of time as James's revision timetable, but has two major advantages:

1) Each subject is covered three times, rather than just once
2) Each subject is covered closer to the exams, so that content will be digested and remembered

Using this method also puts greater pressure on you to revise from a psychological perspective. As James starts to revise Chemistry using the 'standard' revision technique, he has an entire two weeks to revise one subject. Knowing this, it is very easy to procrastinate and say "leave it till tomorrow". However, with the layered learning, time is split up into smaller chunks, which makes it easier to manage, and puts the pressure on getting things done.

As I explained this concept to James, he had the following concern:

James: "Ok, I understand that it would be useful to cover each subject three times instead of just once. But I still only have a small amount of time. How is it possible to cover each subject three times in the amount of time I would usually only finish it once!"

Me: "I split the timetable into layers. Within each layer, each subject is covered once. Notice that 40 days are dedicated to layer one (thorough), 20 days to layer 2 (moderate) and 8 days to layer 3 (brief), thus the number of days are decreasing. Yet in each 'layer' you will be revising the entire subject, start to finish! This is only possible due to the principle of layered learning, <u>where the same</u>

information gets absorbed and retained faster the more layers you complete!"

Things to do 3

Let's test this principle. I would like you to choose a chapter from a text book and read through it as if you were revising and preparing from a book. Leave it for a week, and then read through the chapter again. How much easier was it to grasp and remember the principles? How much less time did you have to spend to learn the same facts? If you repeated this again one week later, you will be able to skim read the chapter in a mere fraction of the time and all the information will come back to you instantly.

The same concept applies for when you get to layer 3 in the layered learning timetable. You should be able to skim read through the book, to jog your memory and it will all come back to you instantly. This is when you know you are fully ready for the exam.

I am now going to tell you exactly what you should be doing in each layer:
- o   Layer 1: Thorough
- o   Layer 2: Moderate
- o   Layer 3: brief

Layer 1: Thorough

The aim of layer 1 is to understand and learn all the material, rather than trying to cram for the exams. During this round, you will have time to go through the harder areas so that you fully understand them.

Layer 1 gives you the freedom to explore areas which you find genuinely interesting, so long as you don't falter away too much from the learning outcomes.

1) Take the core text book and find the learning outcomes
2) Go through each chapter thoroughly. Start with the areas that you haven't covered well in class or you don't understand
3) Spend time learning the principles, using as many resources as you can, including websites, other text books, YouTube, friends and teachers
4) Within each chapter, ask yourself "do I really understand this?". If not, break it down and take your time. It's at this point where time, to an extent, is on your hands

In layer 1, I studied one subject at a time as I wanted to explore each subject as much as possible before moving on to the next one. However, some people have said that they find this method boring and prefer to do a little bit of each subject at a time.

No matter how you do it, the important point is that by the end of layer 1, you should comprehensively understand each subject.

Layer 2: Moderate

Layer 2 focuses on preparing for the exam itself - you should not be covering or trying to understand concepts for the first time! At this point you should have already covered all material once.

1) Read through the entire subject – you should find yourself getting through content a lot faster (approximately 2-3 times the speed) because it will be familiar and you won't be spending time trying to understand new information.

2) Complete a past paper – NOTE: This is usually the hardest attempt, and has more potential for boredom as you are covering details for the second time. However, persevere even if you forget something, you'll get it in the end.

During this round, cover one subject at a time. This is because:

- It will show you the benefits of layer one and illustrate how quickly you can absorb the material the second time round. This will motivate you and increase your confidence.

- Exam timetables can sometimes be crowded and you may only have a few days in between to prepare for each exam. In the worst case scenario you can have multiple exams in a day. For example, a Physics exam in the morning and an English exam in the afternoon. The process of completing one subject at a time will train your mind to group the subject information together and pick it up quickly. Therefore, a few days before the exam, you will be able to skim-read fast enough to cover all the material of each subject.

Once you have completed an entire subject, you are then in a perfect position to start past papers, which must be completed to achieve high marks.

Past papers

Past papers are by far the most effective revision tool. Completing them gets you used to the style of the questions and sometimes the same ones come up again! Having recently revised the entire module, you can focus on your weaker areas and application of concepts. This will also help your timing – the last thing you want is to run out of time during the real thing! You should plan layer 2 so that there is time left for past papers after completing each subject. Aim to complete at least two mock papers within a day – in test conditions.

Layer 3: Weak

Around 1-2 weeks before the exam, you should be ready to start layer 3.

Layer 3 is crucial in gaining the most marks you can. It will ensure that information is fresh in your mind. Often students get tired at this point. However, I urge you to persevere and remember why you are doing this. The last few chapters within this book will help give you that push to continue.

At any point during your revision when you are struggling, say to yourself: "in just x amount of days, I will be free to do as I please, with no associated feelings of guilt. I will sacrifice these days to reap a huge reward."

Look at the goals you stuck on the wall when you started this book.

At this stage you should NOT be learning any new material. Your time is best spent re-reading the majority that you have learned well, rather than trying to cram in a minority that you have not learned well. These days are used to re-familiarise yourself with the information that you already know, so that it is in the forefront of your mind ready to blast out with ease on the day of the exam.

Skim read the content

One skim-read should include going through:
- the main 'core or exam-board textbook'
- any notes you have made
- skim reading your mock papers and mark schemes

As you have already covered all this twice previously, you will be surprised at how fast get through the information and how much you retain!

I feel that layer 3 is really the 'make or break' round, but most importantly it is a layer which is dependent on the first two layers being completed. The important point here is that you are only skim-reading. You are running through all the information as efficiently as you can, so that it jolts your memory and brings all the information to the forefront of your mind.

Subject study order – not what you'd expect

Within layer 3, it is important to choose which subjects to study first and last. Have a look at your exam timetable. Say for example, your exams are in the following order: Chemistry, Biology, German, French. You should work backwards and skim read French, then German, Biology and finally Chemistry. You want to end on Chemistry so that you are not skim-reading and bringing German to the forefront of your mind right before your Chemistry exam!

Days between exams

There may also be 1-2 days between each exam. Push to fit in a smaller fourth skim read to reinforce further, particularly for those subjects at the end of the exam timetable.

The day before the exam

On the day before the exam, you may skim-read if you feel it is necessary. Ideally, you should be in a position where you have already skim-read the information before, and you are simply almost waiting for the exam to come. Even if you feel unprepared, *do not* stress yourself out. At this point, there is little you can do to make a difference for your mark anyway. Believe me, the information is all in there somewhere.

It takes a lot of faith to step back from the books on the evening before your exam, so I don't blame you for feeling anxious. I often became paranoid about forgetting odd details and kept opening my textbook to find that I hadn't.

It's only after university that I realised how a quick skim-read can reduce paranoia and calm nerves. Just remember that if you have followed the above steps carefully, you will do fine.

Although I often get stressed before an exam, I always make sure that I have a good night's sleep. *Do not* attempt the all-nighter. It will not put you in good stead for the rest of the exams. That means no pro-plus too!

A good night sleep is crucial!

Summary of the layers

Layer 1 2/3 of time left before 10 days to exam	Cover each subject <u>slowly, and in detail</u> <u>Start with your weakest areas</u>
Layer 2 1/3 of time left before 10 days to exam	Cover each subject again at 2-3 times the speed of round 1 One subject at a time Complete mock papers immediately after finishing subject
Layer 3 10 days-exam	Spend one day for entire subject <u>Absolutely no</u> new material should be learnt Skim-Read to remind yourself of material Work backwards: Start with the subject of your last exam and finish with your first
Before exam	SKIM READ ONLY Rest

When should I start "The layered learning revision" plan?

James, my cousin who I mentioned earlier, only had 80 days left to start his revision plan. But while it's very easy for me to tell you to start the layered learning revision timetable as early as possible, in reality it may not be that easy. However, you have to keep reminding yourself that A-Level term time isn't very long. To make the year as enjoyable as possible, with as little stress and to also achieve the highest grades, starting as early as you can is the best advice I could give you.

Planning your layered learning revision timetable

When planning your revision timetable, you should use the following approach:

1) Work out how long you have before your first exam.
2) Allocate the last 2 weeks before your exams to layer 3.
3) Between now and your first exam, $2/3^{rd}$ of the time left should be dedicated to completing layer 1. $1/3^{rd}$ of the time left should be dedicated to completing layer 2.

Covering the subjects in the layers, as discussed above, is crucial to achieving high grades. Due to exam pressure, layer 3 will always be stressful no matter how early you have completed layer 1 and layer 2. However, layer 1 and layer 2 can be so much more relaxed, enjoyable and less stressful the earlier you start.

Learning the material can become interesting

Whilst studying for my A-Levels, I started layer 1 very early and remember reading in my Physics text book something about the size of the universe. I spent hours on YouTube trying to truly understand and contemplate the actual size of the universe. In hindsight, it was probably a complete waste of an entire evening but I enjoyed it and could afford to spend time exploring such topics as I had started the layer early.

When used properly, layer 1 is not just for exams. It defines the purpose why we study in the first place – to learn and become knowledgeable and not solely for the purpose of exams. It gives us a time to be inquisitive and ask "why?"

What about homework?

There were many occasions where I ignored homework set by teachers to continue working on my layers. It frustrated everyone, but after explaining my plan, some of my teachers were actually quite supportive. The ones that weren't convinced, eventually gave up trying to chase me for homework and let me get on with it.

I'm not advising you to ignore your homework, but if you do find yourself falling behind don't be afraid to take matters into your own hands. Incorporating a 'power layer' into your revision time table is the perfect way to do this.

The power layer

Having flopped my AS levels during a time when they contributed to 50% of my A-Level grade, I needed to retake almost all of those exams the following year. This amounted to over 20 exams in June. Yes, 20 exams!

Initially my plan was to wait for my teachers to cover all the second year topics in class and then start my first layer. However, I quickly realised this wouldn't work because they were going too slow. At this pace, most of my teachers would finish teaching by late April! This didn't leave enough time to complete first layers for all the second year topics. I had no choice but to take matters into my own hands and work through the syllabus faster than my teachers.

I picked one chunk of the syllabus from each subject and revised them (1st layer) in my spare time before any of my teachers taught them in class.

When my teachers eventually caught up with me, I kind of had an idea about what was going on. Every lesson, I waited for the teacher to begin a topic then scribbled down what I could remember about it. I didn't bother taking notes. I just listened, reaffirmed what I already had stored in my brain and tried to answer any questions.

This process of covering the material before it is taught, then re-affirming it using lessons, is what I refer to as a power layer. I did this for four of my exams. Astonishingly, without recapping any information, I was able to achieve 50-60% on mock papers three months after completing the power layers. On average, those exams I prepared for using the power layer were also the ones I scored highest in. Why? Because the information was absorbed through two different mediums...

1. Writing and reading during self-study
2. Listening and speaking in class

After completing the power layer, another layer closer to exams will take half the time. Don't be surprised if you achieve above 90% in the exams you prepare for in this way. Here's what I suggest...

1.   Complete at least one power layer per subject

I know what you are thinking. 'Is this guy serious? He wants me to revise for an exam on my own before the teacher has even taught anything about it?' It's possible and necessary in my opinion, particularly if you are taking more than 3 A-Levels.

You will find that no one in your year will be doing this. Unfortunately, this is exactly what is required if you want to really improve your chances of achieving A's or even A*'s. If you are able to go against the grain and execute my advice you will achieve grades far beyond your expectations. Trust me and do it!

Don't forget...

With the new linear system, the exams are more like synoptic papers where they assess all your knowledge from the different modules across the two years. This means it's a good idea to get the facts in your head so that you only need to focus on understanding the content in lessons.

2. Get the teaching plan early

Tell your teachers about the power layer and your revision time table. Ask them for their teaching plans. If you are starting in your first year, find out which parts of the syllabus they are teaching after January and start your first layers in those topics now.

Likewise, if you have finished first year, get your hands on next year's lesson schedule. You then have the option to complete multiple first layers in the summer. Edward, one of my mentees completed his four first layers over the summer by working 3-4 hours a day. He whizzed through homework set in those topics and eventually achieved a full set of A*s. Ed initially found working during summer depressing and mind numbing. However, he forced himself into a routine by starting the moment he woke up. Without giving himself time to become distracted, he got his bum on the chair and stayed there. No brushing. No breakfast. No shower, until he was done. Then he was free to enjoy his day, which ended up starting at the same time his mates woke up due to summer holiday lie ins!

3. Focus on past papers rather than final layers if you run out of time

If you find yourself short of time closer to the exam, drop the layered learning time table and focus on past papers. Although not ideal, there are still ways to get the best mark you can. If you are 1 or 2 days away from an exam and haven't completed a 2nd or 3rd layer, then focus on completing <u>all</u> the past papers. It is more important that you have exam practice, and get into the mode of answering questions, before sitting an exam. If your first layer was strong, then completing the past papers should enable you to retain enough to tip your grade above 80%.

The same goes for if you haven't completed your first layer in time. Drop everything and just do exam papers. This should be enough to tip your grade above 50 - 60%.

4. Use your free periods, evenings and weekends.

If you are doing more than 2 A-Levels, you will have to make full use of your free time. More exams mean more study time. There is no way around this!

Think about these assumptions...

"It's Friday night. I can't work on a Friday night"

"It's Sunday. That's a rest day so I'll start tomorrow"

"It's late now so nothing will stick in my mind"

When you think about it, there is no basis for these assumptions. They are made up! Always make an attempt to sit down and hit your targets even if it means squeezing in an hour or two before going out on a Friday night.

Is the layered learning revision timetable really possible?

People have often asked me whether the layered learning revision timetable is an impossible task.

I usually tell them about my university years. In university, the amount of information that you have to learn is immense. There are no clear learning outcomes like during A-Levels. You are expected to read books and books of information throughout the year. The exams are often all huddled within the space of 2-3 days. The concept of successfully completing round 2 and 3 becomes even more impossible: the sheer amount of information means that it is physically impossible to 'skim read' an entire subject in a week, let alone 2-3 days!

Despite this, the process itself of attempting layers 1, 2 and 3 whilst in university made me realise that, during A-Levels, it is definitely possible. It's only after university that you'll realise how easy you had it at A-Level. Ask some of your university friends what they think if you don't believe me!

Have faith in this system. Follow my steps and you will achieve the grades you desire.

What to revise

So far, we have identified exactly when to revise and how best to plan your revision timetable. So, what do you need to revise during the layered learning revision timetable?

1) Learning specification
2) Past exam questions and mark scheme
3) Core text book (obviously!)

The learning specification

The learning specifications are the most valuable texts available to you during your A-Levels. It always surprises me how few people actually look at this!

Before you start revising, print out your learning specification. Read through and familiarise yourself with what is expected of you to pass. More importantly, you can use it to take control of your own learning and save time by ensuring you learn what is actually required.

Going back to the layered learning timetable, you should plan your learning in accordance to what is detailed in the learning outcomes. Each specification is different, but each will tell you exactly what is required.

Some examining bodies provide detailed learning outcomes while others give more of a general overview. Specifications which are less detailed are often in subjects where exams are more essay-based. Although not as specific, do not be put off. You can still use it as a guide to ensure that you cover the subject area of any material that can be tested. It may be of relevance here to ask your teacher for further guidance as to what specifically is expected of you and what level of knowledge is required.

It is also important to look carefully at the language used when describing a learning outcome. This provides valuable clues as to what the examiner expects from you. For example, you will notice a lot of outcomes use a lot of the following words:

1) Describe
2) Explain
3) Define
4) Discuss
5) Distinguish

Past exam questions and mark scheme

When it comes to past papers, I agree with the advice given by most school and teachers. The best way is to recreate exam conditions in your house, conduct the exam under a time limit, mark yourself harshly and correct what you get wrong.

Whenever students ask me how to get A's at A-Level, my short answer is always use past papers. I put just as much emphasis on past papers as I do with text books because:

1. They help calm nerves and fear of taking exams by imitating exam conditions. Nervousness can sometimes be a good thing because of the adrenaline rush, but most of the time it has a negative effect. Our minds don't work at full capacity when there is emotional churning going on. Most of the time we feel nervous because of uncertainty; not knowing what is going to come up and fear of not remembering. My teachers used to say that if you complete past papers and mark yourself properly, the average mark of the last 3 papers will probably be the result you get in the real exam. This rule of thumb held true for me and probably will for you. Therefore, you can

pretty much predict what you're going to get in the exam before you sit it and reduce that debilitating uncertainty.

2. Occasionally questions are changed slightly and repeated. Therefore, you can lock down those marks quickly and spend time on new questions.

3. Completing all the available past papers essentially adds an extra layer before real exams.

Predicting exam questions – the crystal ball approach

Many students compare past papers to try and pick out patterns and predict what questions will come up in the exam. Teachers usually recommend against this saying it's risky and difficult to predict anything because of how large syllabuses are. They are probably right but it still didn't stop me and many others from doing it. However, for any given module, it's more risky if you make predictions before properly completing 1 or 2 layers. This is because it will be easy to convince yourself that certain questions will come up and you'll open up the chance of selectively learn those parts, while neglecting everything else. If you are going to take this crystal ball approach, then I recommend doing it late in the revision process and completing an extra quick rep of those topics you think will come up.

The mark schemes give you the structure of the answer they will expect of you in the exam. In a lot of subjects, students often miss marks not because of lack of knowledge, but because they did not know what the examiner is looking for. So, moral of the chapter – go through the syllabus and mark scheme!

Note taking...Is it worth it?

In university note taking is important because your lecturers write your exam questions. It would be stupid not to record what they talk about. However, during A-Levels, your exams are written by exam boards who, in most cases, base them off their own text books.

During 6th form I found that note taking was used in two different scenarios; studying on your own and during class. The first scenario is when you take notes during independent study to summarise content, in text books or revision guides, with the intention to use them later for revision. In the second scenario, notes are taken from explanations through a teacher dictating from the white board, slides or power-point presentations.

Although some people benefit from note taking, I never did and nor did anyone of the people who I have taught my method to. I always thought it consumed too much energy and was a waste of time. It also encourages procrastination. Ask yourself, did you go and get lots of coloured pens or little que cards 'in preparation' to take notes?! What is the point of spending loads of time writing neat notes, or loads of illegible notes, with colourful diagrams, tip-exing all the mistakes and filing them away when you can just read the textbook!?

The main purpose of note taking is essentially to ensure you read the book without getting bored or distracted. The other reason is to consolidate information in your core text book into a simpler format. This means that you can re-revise directly from your notes. The benefit of note taking, if done properly, is that you may find it easier to revise from your own notes, because they are in your own words. However, you have to ask yourself:

For the amount of extra time you have to spend preparing these notes, is it worth it?

When taking notes it's easy to fool yourself into thinking you've done a lot of work when you haven't actually learnt much at all. I've met many students who feel copying out of a text book is a way of learning and also a valid way of completing a layer. I'm sorry to say, this is simply not true.

Don't fall into the trap of studying to simply say you did x hours of work today, making yourself feel good. Ask yourself what have you learnt? It's better to do one hour of revision and take 2 things in, rather than 5 hours and take in nothing!

Why?

Well, these notes have to be continuously organised therefore, wasting even more time when you could be doing another layer. For biology, physics and maths I just used the module text book taking no notes at all.

Passive note taking is like writing on a typewriter without the keys making contact with the page – lots of effort and time spent but nothing retained.

In most cases the exam-board text books are presented in a clear and concise way, so there is no need to do any summarising or bullet pointing. <u>Learning directly from them is all that is required to get high A's</u>.

It is important to note that some exam boards put more emphasis on the syllabus, provide a limited amount of learning texts and leave it to schools to provide the correct material for students. For these subjects, <u>note taking will be important</u> and should be used in conjunction with the techniques explained in this section. These subjects include English, Politics, Economics, Psychology and generally those that are examined in an essay format.

If I don't make notes, how do I revise?

For fact based and short answer question exams, note taking, both during class and self study, is a very inefficient way of revision. This is one of those points in the book where you need to be open minded, because you've probably been hearing different things from your teachers for quite a while. For these subjects, to get close to 100%, all you need from start to finish are the **exam-board text books** and **past papers**. You do not need to waste time writing colourful notes with diagrams all filed in order. All you need to use is the **scribble technique...**

What is the scribble technique?

Scribble Technique

| Open Your Text Book |

| Read through 1 – 2 sides |

| Close the book |

| Scribble down everything you can remember |

| Open the book and see what <u>you forgot/got wrong</u> |

| Read next 1-2 sides and repeat |

That is all you need to do! I did this for all of my biology modules and hit above 90% for almost all of them.

Scribble technique vs traditional note taking: which one is better?

Traditional Note Taking refers to producing summarised notes using exam board text books/classroom study and using these for revision closer to the exam.

Conversely, the scribble technique is superior to any form of note taking because it is a:

1. More effective way of holding facts in your memory for a longer period of time
2. Faster way of absorbing large volumes of information

With the scribble technique you are not concerned with using the notes later and are focusing on learning material there and then. Focusing on memorising and learning the material, means you'll be happy to make mistakes and forget things when scribbling because you will open the page again and see what you got wrong or missed. The constant process of making mistakes and correcting them helps you retain information in a much faster and superior way to standard note taking.

To further explain, when you are trying to remember information to scribble down you will forget things. This will bother you in the same way it would if you forgot a song name that you wanted to download. When that song name pops into your head what do you experience? Probably a short pointless moment of joy! Chances are that song name will be nicely stuck in your memory from that point onwards.

Affective memory retention is all about creating those pointless moments of joy after challenging yourself to remember something.

I know it just sounds silly, but you will realise its effectiveness if you try it.

If you don't remember the fact then that's fine because shortly you will find out (when you open the textbook to check), and instead of thinking "Aha!" you will say "I knew it!". It has a similar level of effectiveness but obviously the more you remember on your first go the better. Treat the scribble technique as a game of 'How much can I remember?'

If we assume the text book holds 100% of the syllabus, then memorising even 70% of the text book is better than memorising 100% of your notes which only hold a summarised portion of the syllabus. Appendix 1 explains this in more detail. It compares the two techniques by looking at the time taken to absorb information and the retention of material (how long it stays in your brain for).

Scribble technique? Don't be Silly

"Are you having a laugh? Surely you're not suggesting actually memorising straight from textbooks?"

This is usually the response I get when suggesting the scribble technique. Believe me I know what you're thinking because I reacted the same way when I first heard about it. What changed my mind was finding out that everyone who learnt in this way were not only hitting A's but high marks reaching above 90%. Those who made concise, neat, organised, time consuming notes and used summarised revision guides were usually in the B and C range. It may be hard at first, but persevere.

"There is no way I can remember that much. Isn't that why we are told to take notes and summarise the key points in text books?"

You will be surprised how much you remember. I spontaneously did a biology past paper 2 months after completing a strong first rep and hit 62%. I can't put this down to luck as I got similar marks when I tried two more papers. After completing further faster layers closer to exam time I bumped up my final exam mark to 96%.

"I know people who are note takers and got As"

I'm not arguing that traditional note taking doesn't work, I'm saying that using the scribble technique using text books works better because you learn directly using exam board information in a highly time efficient way.

"This is way too time consuming and I won't finish in time"

Overall time spent is actually lower when using the scribble technique because reading and scribbling takes less time than writing neatly. So the rate you cover material is higher (see Appendix 1). On the first layer for my biology modules I could usually cover 10 – 12 A4 sides an hour. On the last layer, just before the exam, I could effectively cover 20+ sides an hour.

Revision guides: are they worth it?

Revision guides are beautiful. They are small, selective, colourful, filled with pretty pictures and promise to cover the entire A-Level curriculum in twenty pages.

They don't.

They try to filter the thicker exam-board text books into thin bullet pointed, diagrammatical and colourful pieces of text, but they miss out valuable bits of information which distinguishes an A and C grade student.

Remember that the core textbooks are written by the exam boards. They are written in the same language that you will need to use to answer the various exam questions.

In my first year, I remember seeing my boring looking thick biology text book next to a thin colourful revision guide on the table and thinking "surely I don't need to read all that". I paid the price. While it may seem like a lot of hard work, it will be worth it.

Revision guides can be used as something to browse through in addition to your core textbook, but should never be used alone. They are an aid, not a substitute.

Comparing the most popular learning methods

To summarise, I've compared the scribble technique with two of the most popular forms of revision.

1. Summarised Revision Guide – Learning straight out of revision guides.
2. Note Taking + Later Learning – Taking notes from text books and using them to revise near exams.

The table below compares these two techniques with the scribble technique using three barometers.

-   **Time:** looks at the total time it will take for you to achieve an A or above in any given module exam.
-   **Efficiency:** tests the volume of information you can effectively absorb per hour/day/week of studying.
-   **Retention:** assesses the volume of information held in your memory and the length of time it stays there for.

Overall Effectiveness: The last row states the overall effectiveness of each method based on all the three barometers.

	Summarised Rev. Guide	Note Taking + revising from notes	Scribble Technique from Core Text book
Time	Low	High	Average-High
Efficiency	Good	Poor	Good
Retention	Poor	Average	Good
Overall Effectiveness	Low	Average	High

From this table, you can see that using the scribble technique overall is favoured and scores high in time, efficiency and retention. Everyone's different, and everyone works differently, but if your current method is failing you, we would advise you to give the scribble technique a try.

Type of subjects and how to revise for them

For A-Levels I have split the subject types into three categories based on the way in which you need to answer exam questions. The most popular A-Level subjects have been categorised in the table.

Fact recall – The subjects that come under this category generally have large volumes of facts which you will need to memorise and recall in the exam.

Method and understanding – These subjects require understanding, practice and a relatively small amount of fact learning.

Written prose – Subjects that require the ability to convert facts and opinions into written prose.

Subject	Fact Recall	Method & Understanding	Written Prose
English			•
Mathematics	•	•	
Biological Sciences	•		
Psychology	•		•
History			•
Chemistry	•	•	
General Studies			•
Physics	•	•	
Geography	•		
Sociology	•		•
Business Studies		•	
Media/Film/TV Studies			•
Religious Studies			•
Design and Technology	•		
Physical Education	•		
Economics	•		
Government & Politics	•		•

As you see from the table, these categories can overlap. However, it is generally easy to distinguish between them. Each category requires a different method for learning and preparation throughout the year for the final exam. For a subject like Physics, where you have an equal amount of fact-learning and method-understanding, a combination of techniques can be used. The section below will explain the optimum methods for each category based on research and my own experience.

Fact recall subjects

How to revise on your own?

For these subjects, use the scribble technique with your exam board text books. Remember as you are reading the information from the text book, work hard at understanding the material as well.

What to do in class?

Have you ever had a really bad teacher and you just sit there thinking, this is a waste of time? Well classroom time can be extremely beneficial or it can just go to waste. Remember, you have to be at school and you have to sit in that classroom. Make the most of it! Later you can use the time you have saved to have fun or relax.

Classroom lessons should be treated as a layer. Whether you're seeing the material for the first time, or you're going over something you've seen before, the best way to make use of that classroom time is to be interactive with the teacher (answer/ask questions). More importantly, focus on understanding and memorising the material.

In addition to doing multiple layers, absorbing information through different channels improves the ability to retain content. These channels are reading, writing, speaking, hearing and doing. By being interactive in class you use all these channels at once.

Method & understanding subjects

How to revise on your own?

For method subjects like maths, the general advice that most teachers preach is practice, practice, practice. I agree whole heartedly with this. Intelligence and a certain analytical mind can help with these subjects but this is by no means a prerequisite. **The person who completes the most number of practice questions before the exam will usually get the higher mark – it's as simple as that.**

Maths mechanics was the first module I properly revised for after receiving my AS grades (I got a D). I was massively upset from my results and was feeling insecure and annoyed about not being 'smart enough' to do well. I felt like I had nothing to lose and wanted to prove a point to myself. I remember saying the following in front of the mirror: "If I do every single question in this Mechanics 1 text book and still don't get an A then it would truly prove I'm not cut out for this". Over the remainder of the summer holidays I kept my word and completed every single question in that text book and worked through the answers. I used my classroom lessons as a strong 2nd layer of the module (power layer) and surprised both myself and my teacher with regard to how much I knew. That day I realised, I didn't get a D because I wasn't smart enough, it was because I wasn't practicing enough or revising properly.

As the exam period approached, and with multiple exams either side of maths mechanics, I only had one day to recap the module. I was worried that I would forget all the content I'd spent my summer learning, after all it was four months ago! However, the first 2 layers were strong and I was shocked when I hit 91% in the exam.

I realised that learning in layers was the way forward, and while it seemed laborious, having cut out the time of making notes and faffing about in class, getting down to it and learning right from the start actually worked. The penny had well and truly dropped. From then I swore by the power of solid practice combined with repetition or layered learning.

Textbooks

Most textbooks provided by exam boards usually have answers to practice questions at the back of the book. If they don't it's important that you get them from your teachers. However, if you get stuck on a question it is critical that you don't look at the answer too quickly. Be stubborn and personally insulted by the fact you can't figure it out using your head; keep pounding at the question until you're exhausted. It's more beneficial if you come up with an answer and then check if it's right (even if your answer is wrong).

I remember occasions when I became extremely stubborn, refused to look at answers and minced at individual questions for long periods of time (sometimes more than an hour). This was very extreme and you don't need to do that but I thought it was worth emphasising.

In a similar way to the scribble technique described earlier, the process of pounding at a question and then having that 'light bulb moment' will create a strong memory. If that question comes up in the exam you will remind yourself and think "This is that question which took me ages to figure out". **The more questions you do and the more stubborn you are with completing them without help, the better chance you are giving yourself of remembering what to do in the exam.**

What to do in class?

With these subjects, focusing in lessons can really boost your grades. This is because there are a bunch of tricks and short cuts which can make your life easier in the exam. Your teachers should show you these in class, so it would be a good idea to have a few sets of notes outlining all the important hints and tips. What you don't want is pages and pages of classroom notes with different examples explaining the same thing.

Written prose subjects

How to revise on your own?

You might be thinking "I study English and Psychology I can't just memorise the whole text book, I'll be told off for plagiarism". It's true, elements which you'll be tested on, such as fluency of expression and vocabulary, cannot be learnt using this method. But that's only a small piece of the puzzle. While prose subjects are different to more factual based subjects, to achieve an A grade, memory plays a massive part – approximately 40-50%.

Having interviewed a number of students who have taken essay-based exams (like economics, business studies, English, psychology and politics), the part where they fall down is remembering everything they want to say. There are so many things to think about; grammar, structure, flow, application to the question, referencing. This, coupled with the amount to write, (students write on average 8 A4 sides for English A-Levels in a 3 hours exam) can sometimes result in failure.

These subjects are based on application and analysis, theory past papers and formulating a structure for your essays is imperative. Therefore, the scribble technique will help you learn the theoretical elements of the syllabus. This will save you a lot of time in the exam as it will allow you to focus more on your analysis.

What differentiates A grade students from C grade students is the ability to analyse the question and contrast or apply it to existing academic theory (which is available through the syllabus). The scribble technique will help you learn the theory in the syllabus so that all you have to worry about during the exam is your own analysis. Now I'm sure you'll agree that knowing a number of theories off the top of your head, which you can apply to your own analysis when time is of the essence – is sure to be very helpful.

There are 5 key areas which are examined in written prose exams. The table below describes them and shows where the scribble technique can be used.

Key Area	What it is?	Scribble technique?
State your point	A relevant statement that helps directly answer the question using theory learnt using the text book	Yes – syllabus learnt through text book
Quote	Quote from your given text or an author	Yes – provide evidence to your point through referencing – this will help you gain extra marks
Comment	Analysis – effect of language on reader, explore and discuss what the evidence shows	Yes – this is from your syllabus
Punctuation & Grammar	Not something you can memorise for the exam	No – not directly for the exam
Structure	The flow of the essay	No

What to do in class?

Written prose subjects are unique in that the exams marks are subjective to the marker. Experienced teachers often know what the examiners are looking for and can provide valuable advice during lessons. Make an effort to be involved and listen to your teachers during lessons.

Mind mapping – mental filing system

Much of this chapter has explored the details of study technique. I would now like to take a step away from this and discuss the importance of keeping an eye on the bigger picture when it comes to learning the material for each module. What do I mean by this? It's very easy to become so bogged down in detail, that when it comes to exam questions, you struggle to recall the correct information or become mixed up with other things you have learnt.

You can tackle this by practicing past papers, but you also need to have an organised thought process so that you can pick out the correct pieces of information stored in your memory. Here's where things can go wrong. If you've focused on the details too much during your revision/layers, the organisation of that information in your mind may be poor. This can result in confusion during exams.

Let me give you an example...

In maths there are many methods that are similar; without proper mind mapping you can accidently use one method when you're supposed to use another. Integration and differentiation are an example of such a scenario. These methods are used in calculus and using one instead of the other can result in completely the wrong answer.

Most people, including myself, create these mental mind-maps naturally while revising. However, I've come across some students who don't. Usually if a student with strong motivation and good revision technique underachieves, it's usually because of poor mind mapping.

Good Vs poor mind mapping

The best way to gauge your mind mapping skills are to analyse how you link any given exam/practice question to the information required to answer it (in your memory bank). The diagrams below show the thought processes of a good and poor mind mapper:

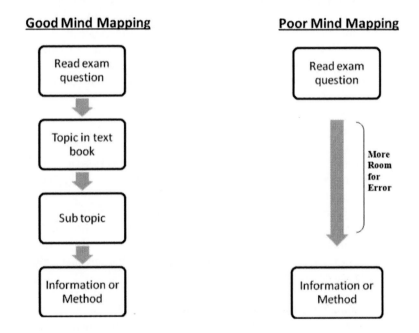

As you can see a good mind mapper not only learns the information or method, but also has an idea of what topic or chapter it falls under. Therefore the topics are categorised and you create clear dividing lines that leave less room for error and helps avoid mixing things up.

At first glance, the process diagram for 'Poor Mind Mapping' seems quite efficient. However, it leaves more room for error and you could end up recalling accurate information or methods but from the incorrect topic.

Are you a natural mind mapper?

You can identify if you are naturally good at mind mapping if you bring up topic/chapter names during general conversation. For example, a Psychology student while discussing a module with his/her mates would probably ask questions like 'is that from chapter 4?' or 'didn't we cover that during that Cognitive Psychology lesson a few weeks back?' You can always tell when someone doesn't mind map because when you mention the names of certain topics or chapter headings, they usually have a blank look on their face.

If you don't naturally mind map, what can you do?

During A-Levels I unintentionally mind mapped as I was revising. After the first layer of a subject, I could usually think of a piece of information, open up my textbook and pick out the chapter it was in. In some cases I could remember the actual page. You might be thinking... surely that is difficult to do? The answer is no – not if you adopt certain habits during your study cycle. These habits are regular reviewing material, reaffirming topics and physical mind mapping.

Regularly reviewing previous material
Every time you finish a study session in your mind briefly go over the information you have covered, summarise it into a few lines and remind yourself of the topic and/or subtopic it falls under. Repeat this on a day-to-day basis when you sit down and start to

study for the same module again. This shouldn't take more than a couple of minutes.

Reaffirming topics

Be the person who knows all the names to the chapters and topics. Talk about the chapters out loud when discussing with friends or teachers to reaffirm them. When you're in lessons and the teacher brings up a topic, think about the summaries you have made during self study.

Physical mind mapping

Physically drawing out mind maps can be very beneficial. If you haven't come across them before here's an example of one for A-Level Physics.

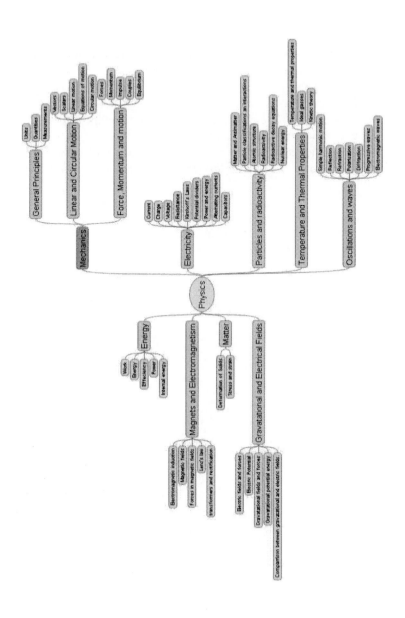

Before the actual exam use the mind map as a guide and run through in your mind the topics and summarisations you've made for them.

Mind mapping tutorial

These days there are some apps and websites that help you build mind maps. However, I recommend doing it the old fashioned way and just drawing them out on an A4 or A3 piece of paper.

Step 1: Write your topic or subject name at the centre of the page.

Step 2: Choose the labels for the first layer of branches. If you have a good exam textbook then it's best to use the chapter headings. If not, then use headings in your syllabus.

Step 3: Draw out branches to key topics under each chapter.

Given that we want the mind map to show an overview of a subject or module, I wouldn't produce any further branches. As you read over your mind map think through or jot down on a piece of paper the important details that fall under each topic.

Synoptic papers

These internal mind maps and chain reaction processes are crucial now that we are back to the linear exam system or if you still have synoptic exams. Not only will you need to consider individual topics, but you'll also have to distinguish between all the topics you have covered over the two years.

Your thought process should follow this path...

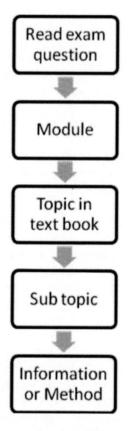

In my own experience, I never consciously or physically made a mind map. However, by thoroughly reviewing topics and spending large amounts of time on chapters, I naturally made my own mental filing system. If you find that you are unable to do this, you must make a conscious effort to do so. Take time out from your study cycle and physically write out mind maps.

This skill will become massively beneficial when you hit university as information from different modules (not topics) can overlap. Effective mind mapping will save a significant amount of time.

Study leave...how to make the most of it?

Hopefully by the time study leave arrives, you will have completed at least one layer for each subject. If you have, then give yourself a pat on the back because you are well on your way to achieving top grades! Now all you need to do is complete one or two further layers and past papers before everything kicks off. This is a testing time and you have to try and stay productive throughout the day.

Here are some hints on what you can do to maximise your work rate:

1. Regularly change environment – After a few hours of working in the same spot it's helpful to move somewhere else. Psychologically you will be 'starting fresh' again. I personally like spending one half of the day at home and then walking to the library to finish the rest.

2. Avoid heavy meals – You feel tired after a large meal because all the blood rushes away from your head to your stomach. A heavy meal might mean a few hours of low productivity.

3. Manage your stress – Our minds don't work too well when there's a whole load of emotional churning going on. When you're exhausted at the end of each day, do something that lowers your stress such as exercise, TV, video games or chatting to mates.

4. Work under bright white light – There are two main types of indoor lighting; bright white and warm white. Warm white is generally used for living conditions to create comfortable 'easy on the eyes' lighting while bright light is used in offices to imitate daylight conditions and increase productivity. Try and work during daylight hours or in places where there are bright white lights.

Try and take each day at a time, don't worry and do whatever suits you!

Bag of tricks...alternative memory techniques

Occasionally for some exam questions you have to memorise information in the form of an item list or a process. For example, in biology, transcription is a process whereby a protein molecule is built in a cell. This process has 6 steps which students will need to remember for the exam. Usually, layered learning and the scribble technique are powerful enough to commit this information to memory. However, it doesn't hurt to have a few more tricks up your sleeve. This is to really make sure you remember all you need in the exam.

Our minds can only remember a limited number of items at a time and even after several layers, some information is awkward and arduous to memorise. Mnemonics and picture association are useful aids for these scenarios. Let's have a look at them...

Picture association

This technique involves creating memory triggers by first associating objects with numbers and then the objects with information we want to learn. Our minds find it easier to remember objects and scenarios than numbers or facts. Therefore, we can use an object to create a mental link between the items of information we want to learn and the corresponding item number.

86

This technique is not only useful for an item list which has to be remembered in a consecutive order, but also if you need to call upon a specific item or number.

For example, earlier I mentioned the transcription process most biology students need to learn. In step 2 of the transcription process, an enzyme called RNA polymerase unwinds and unlinks the two strands of DNA. In the exam you may have to recall this specific step or know where this step occurs in the process. With picture association you can easily remember the object associated with the step no. and therefore remember the information associated with the object.

Picture association tutorial:

Step 1: Assign memorable objects to numbers 1 – 15. Use the ones we have here.

Number	Object	Reason
1	Tree	1 tree stands alone
2	Light Switch	2 options: on and off
3	Traffic Light	3 options: green, amber and red
4	Dog	A dog has 4 legs
5	Glove	A glove has 5 fingers
6	Devil	The devil's number is 666
7	Heaven	7 rhymes with heaven
8	Skate	8 rhymes with skate
9	Cat	A cat has 9 lives
10	Bowling Ball	10 pin bowling
11	Twin Towers	September 11th attacks and the twin towers looked like 11
12	Eggs	12 Dozen in a pack of eggs
13	Pumpkin	13 is "unlucky" – Halloween – pumpkin
14	Flowers	14th Feb is Valentine's day where you give/receive flowers
15	Cinema Ticket	Only over 15's allowed for some cinema movies

Once you have memorised and associated each number to an object, these objects become **Number Associated Objects**.
This means the number and object are interchangeable – whenever you think of no. 2 you should immediately think "light switch" and vice versa.

<u>Task</u>

    1.   Memorise and scribble down the number, association and object down <u>three</u> times:

...

"2...On & Off...Light Switch"
"3.....Red, Amber & Green....Traffic Light"

...

    2.   Then do it backwards <u>three</u> times:

...

"Light Switch...On & Off...2"
"Traffic Light...Red, Amber and Green...3"

Step 2: Use your imagination to link the **Number Associated Object** to the item of information. You do this by playing out a memorable scenario using your imagination.

For example, for step <u>2</u> in the transcription process, we can imagine the <u>RNA polymerase</u> approaching the DNA strand and pressing a <u>light switch</u> which then causes the <u>DNA to unwind</u>.

This method might sound quite silly but that's exactly why it will stick in your head. It's easier for your mind to remember scenarios or images rather than sentences/numbers and it's even easier if those scenarios are funny or crazy.

Note: When imagining the scenario, close your eyes and make it very vivid and clear. This will help the scenario stick in your memory.

Mnemonic

This is a common technique used to help retain and recall information. Through common sense we can see how they can work well and its effectiveness is backed by studies. In this section we will explain the two most effective types of mnemonics: Music and Expression or Word.

Music

Are you one of those people who can recite song lyrics after only hearing it a handful of times? I personally am not. However, if you are, it's probably because the fundamental systems in your mind are highly sensitive to melody and beat. This can be useful for remembering information.

When I mentioned music mnemonics you probably thought of the "ABC" song used to help primary school kids learn the alphabet. However, although useful, this is not the technique I am referring to. Instead of creating song lyrics out of information, a more efficient way to use your 'musical mind' is to use songs in conjunction with the scribble technique. This can be done by reading (out loud or in your mind) information from your text book in a song like way or like a jingle. You can therefore benefit from combining the highly efficient 'forgetting-remembering' cycle in the scribble technique with the mental links created using your unique musical mind.

Expression or word

Using expression or word mnemonics is a useful memory technique. When memorising a list of items you can produce a word mnemonic using the first letter of each item of information.

For example...in English, to join two clauses together you use coordinating conjunctions. These are for, and, nor, but, or, yet and so. These can be remembered using the word mnemonic FANBOYS. An expression mnemonic can also be used...

For	And	Nor	But	Or	Yet	So
Four	Apples	Nearly	Broke	On	Your	Sidewalk

If you don't want to spend time thinking of mnemonics like these then you can find existing ones online or even using mnemonic calculators on some websites.

In comparison to the scribble technique, both these techniques are much less efficient. Therefore, I do not recommend using these techniques all the time but only for memorising a large number of items or for information that you are struggling to retain even after several layers. Please do not replace the scribble technique with these alternative memory tricks – you will probably run out of time!

5 Step 2 - Study Cycle: am I working hard enough?

This chapter will define and discuss the 'Study Cycle' and look at two assumptions that students commonly make: 1) the misconceptions of hard work and 2) the effect your environment and friends have on your attitude to studying.

How can you tell whether you are doing enough for the exam? We don't have any crystal balls so we have to determine what 'enough' is. To help do this, we provide an example of a student's typical day (before) when he <u>thought</u> he was working hard and (after) when he <u>actually</u> was working hard.

The second assumption touches on the significant impact your friends and environment have on your perception of 'hard work'. Before, discussing these assumptions, I'm first going to define the term 'Study Cycle'.

What is the 'Study Cycle'?

The study cycle is the process you participate in on a day-to-day basis during your academic life. It has three elements which are intent, action and maintenance.

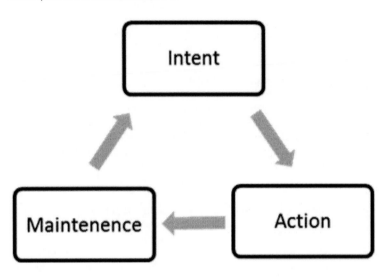

Intent – How often you think about or feel like working?

Action – How often do you act on your intent and start working?

Maintenance – How effectively, and for what length of time do you work for, before needing a break?

We asked three different students (Rachel, Ali and Manos), all with varying A-Level results, about their study cycle and how effective they are at executing each of the three elements. Read the 3 profiles on the next page and see if you can relate to any of them.

	Rachel - A*/A	Ali - B/C	Manos - D or less
Intent	During most free periods, evenings and weekends I have the inclination to get to a table and work. The idea of doing work runs through my head quite often.	Studying during my free time isn't always a priority. I usually just go with the flow and spend time with mates. It's really closer to exam time when I think about it more.	I quite often think I should be working but something always holds me back.
Action	I do not have a problem getting to the table during the time I am not in lessons. In 80% of the instances when I 'talk the talk' I 'walk the walk'.	On the days that I do get the inclination to work I often procrastinate. I easily convince myself out of studying, only really sitting down and working effectively half of the time.	Starting work is a bit of a problem, but then when I finally do attempt something I can concentrate – that's until I get stuck.
Maintenance	Once I'm on the table I can usually jot down some goals and get stuck in. I do get distracted every few minutes but it's not long before I'm reading the next paragraph. After 15-20 mins when my attentions span is low I might walk around, play on my phone or get a snack but after 5-10 mins feel the need to sit back down, glimpse at my goals and do some more revision	On the occasions I do get on a table to work I am actually quite effective, especially closer to exams. Aside from the odd distraction or loss of concentration I can hit my targets if I'm in the right mood. Whether I'll be able to do it again tomorrow is another story.	As soon as I get stuck on something I start to procrastinate or give up. If I don't get it now I probably won't get it later, I can't be bothered to waste my time. Even closer to exams there are some days where I get to the table once or twice and get a small amount done. Sometimes I think what's the point, I haven't done that much till now, but I'm sure I'll be able to scrape a C – I've been to the majority of my lessons.

Of course there are many more variations than the examples in the table, but it will give you a good idea of the differences in work ethic. You have to be effective in all three study cycle elements across days, weeks and months to become a high performer.

All three students were aiming for high grades and felt they were working hard enough to achieve them. So why were their final grades so different? The answer lies in their perception of 'hard work' and the assumptions they made to shape that perception.

What is hard work? – "But I worked so hard..."

"I worked really hard for my exams particularly for Psychology and I still only scraped Cs"
-Ali

'Hard work' is a common phrase. Have you ever thought about what hard work actually is? You probably hear it all over the place like during assembly, from your teachers and parents. But what exactly is working hard? It's a phrase that is thrown around so much by everyone with very little explanation. I believe that working hard is a skill in itself and the lack of detail about this is one of the main reasons why students misjudge what they need to do to achieve high marks.

Unfortunately, like Ali, I also made the same misjudgement and many others also do. It is for this reason I went on a mission to find out what these high performers like Rachel were doing in their free time. I tried to find out everything about their habits, routines and perception of hard work.

He goes out every night, but yet he gets an A

At college it was tough to balance my social life and my work life. Firstly, I had my parents on my case about staying in and revising. Then, I had my friends constantly asking me to go out. It was hard to find a balance. I obviously wanted to go out, it's tough to stay in and revise when your mates are playing football or at the cinema. However, I used to think if they could do it and get straight As, then so could I; that's where I was wrong. Out of that group of friends 4 got 3 C grades or under (myself included) 3 got Bs and 3 got As.

After receiving my AS level results, I asked my friends about their study patterns and how we differed so drastically. What was most frustrating was that I wouldn't consider myself to be less intelligent in comparison to them. In actual fact I'd say we all had pretty similar intelligence. I soon found out that the difference was how we managed our time.

Looking back it seems quite obvious; you see, after school, I'd get home and have about 3 or 4 hours where I'd have a shower, eat my dinner, do maybe an hour of homework, watch a bit of TV and then get ready to go out. This was where I and some of my friends differed.

I expected them to all be crazy undercover workaholics – they weren't. It seemed most of them just worked for a couple of hours every day. My friend Tom often said "I really need to concentrate and learn the next three chapters so then I can go out and have fun." Their remarks got me thinking about my own habits and how I could change them to help achieve what they did.

After some thought, I realised I had a bad study cycle because I was unaware of how much and how often I needed to work. My ignorance resulted from having certain assumptions that I didn't question. However, once I realised where I was going wrong, I was able to improve my day-to-day habits.

Thinking independently and making small adjustments in attitude helped me become proactive during certain periods of the day. The most significant improvement happened once I changed my habits at home.

Everyone tells you to work hard but most people don't understand what working hard entails. You may think coming home after college, doing your homework and watching TV most of the year is sufficient to get the grade you want. Or that reading over your notes in your free period, spending an hour at home doing text-book exercises and taking the weekend off is sufficient. Simply, it's not.

To help you gauge what course your current routine is on, look at the example of a student I mentored in second year A-Levels. You can see how his mindset changes between AS level and A2 level.

	Typical Day - AS Level Year	Typical Day - A2 Level Year
	Result: ECCD	Result: AAAB
Early Morning	Wake up, get ready, meet mates, catch the train and banter! Finish off any homework due for today using mate's work to copy.	Wake up and type out a few things to get done by the end of the day on phone. Then get ready, meet mates, catch the train and banter.
Lessons	Attend all lessons and sit at the back. Depending on the teacher, joke around or stay quiet and look busy. Usually fairly interactive in class if something interesting comes up and pay some attention to avoid embarrassment if the teacher asks a question.	Attend all lessons and don't really mind where to sit. Now more interactive and treat the lesson as a repetition rather than an hour of boredom! If, through my own repetition, the material taught has only already been covered, try to jot down information off the top of my head to see how much I can remember. Although occasionally, I still annoy the teacher and get in trouble for talking.

Breaks	During the short 20 minute break and the lunch break, usually chill in the common room with mates. Occasionally use the gym and play basketball.	Break time activity depends on productivity the previous day/evening. If I didn't get much done I tend to push myself to hit my targets in the library. However, if level of work need has been satisfied I just end up chatting to mates or playing footy.
Free Periods	Free periods are the best thing in life especially if they are at the end of the day because you can leave early! Usually chill in the common room or finish homework set by strict teachers.	Find a quiet spot somewhere, jot down goals and drill out repetitions. This will give me a bit more free time at home or on the weekend when there's a friends 18th or something I really want to go to

After College	Wait for others to finish up to take the train home together. Sometimes go to the shops or just chill outside school and have a laugh with friends.	If I've hit my targets, relax and spend time with friends. However, I go over the repetition I started in my free period and organise my free time so I can fit in some revision and relaxing. Head to the library or home ASAP!
At Home	Sit on the sofa, turn on the TV and eat dinner. Log into Facebook and catch up on the latest gossip. Spend some time on homework but rarely finish and rely on copying from mates in the morning.	Instead of immediately turning the TV on, I lay out my books and quickly jot down a to-do list. This is just to 'set the theme' of the evening. Over the remainder of the evening I work through my to-do list so I can relax later.

By comparing both days it's clear that in certain parts of the day some changes were more drastic than others. Let's discuss the differences in more detail.

Early morning – I believe something is only a true priority if it's the first thing you think about in the day and the last at night. Noting down a set of goals first thing in the morning, whether it be learning a really hard chapter or simply memorising a page or two, is a great way to reaffirm that your priority is to achieve top grades.

Lessons – From comparing both years in the table, the individual didn't actually change that much as a person. All that changed were his priorities and attitude. We can see that during A2, he didn't get as bored during lessons because his mind was focused on short-term goals and testing himself on how much he knew. Each class was no longer seen as just a boring lesson, but another layer of information to ensure as much as possible was remembered on the exam day.

My personal experience...

A lot of my improvement came as a result of correcting the elements in my study cycle. My change in attitude became most apparent when I was in a class where the teacher struggled to control everyone. During first year, I would be the first to take advantage of these teachers and mess about. However, the following year was different. I would just sit at the back and continue with my layers, only looking up if I heard the word 'exam' (in case there was a hint or tip being said). I was so obsessed with my short-term goals that my concern for completing them outweighed any other background stuff that went on.

If you do this no one will look down on you. If you feel stupid or think your friends will think your 'a loser' or 'not cool' just ask yourself: what's the point of wasting your time for a couple of laughs or maybe even detention when in a couple of years time you will be at university or pursuing a career where you have complete freedom?

Some students react to my advice by saying I want them to turn into workaholic nerds. That's massively far from the truth. I'm encouraging you to be strong minded, not to follow the crowd and make the most of your time – trust me, it will benefit you in the future!

Breaks – They are called breaks for a reason. Switch off your mind, relax and let loose so you're ready to get back to business later.

Free periods – During first year I remember always going to the common room with mates to 'study'. However, this would almost always fizzle out into a relaxed, talkative, 'work' session where barely anything got done. As fun as they were, these group work sessions fooled me into thinking I was working hard when I wasn't. The hundreds of hours wasted probably hurt my final grade.

Free periods are great gaps in the day where you can work on your self-study targets. Thinking you can work effectively near your mates in an unsupervised environment, like a common room or library where your whole year group seem to be is a bad assumption. Again, it's OK to have the one-off free period where you're doing pretty much nothing, but making it a habit will hurt your marks.

After college – For me personally, when comparing my first and second years, there was a huge difference in what I was thinking about after college. During AS I was relieved the day was over, looked forward to going home and watching Eastenders. There was a significant change during second year; I started thinking of exams, how far they were and if I was on track. Because of this I wasn't at all interested in faffing about and just wanted to get home. Keep your eye on the goal.

Identify where or how you get distracted. If you know there are too many distractions at home like chilling out with your brothers or sisters, going on your computer or playing video games, then stay at school or college for an extra two hours.

At home – For me, what I did in those few hours after college made the real difference to my grades. It is the only time where you can control your environment and be alone. For years I developed the habit of coming home and switching on the TV. However, I proactively changed that habit and it stayed that way throughout university and beyond. In my opinion these hours are important and, if used well, you could probably hit high marks even if you muck about during breaks and free periods. Doing this means you won't feel that niggling guilt when you're out with friends, because let's face it, we feel guilty for not studying when we're supposed to – no matter how small.

To ensure I was using this time most efficiently and effectively, I used the appropriate method of learning. This meant working through practice questions and exam-board text books, for 'method' based subjects like maths, and the scribble technique for 'memory' based subjects like biology.

Just to be clear I was no superman and, like everyone else, some days I just wouldn't be able to concentrate. However, across weeks and months the net affect was positive and a lot more was getting done in the right way. On days that I knew I could concentrate and felt really driven to hit my targets, I wouldn't hesitate to step out the house to meet my girlfriend, play footy, play pool or just chill with friends.

Summary
- Make the most of your time – organise yourself. 'Work hard, play hard'
- Keep an eye on your productivity – How many pages are you covering per week?
- Stay focused on your short-term goals.
- Avoid winding down as soon as you get home - push to drill out more pages/ questions.

Measuring your hard work

How do you measure how hard you are working?

It's simple, you have to gauge whether <u>you</u> are being productive, not productive compared to your friends. You have to be productive to your own standards, only you know your boundaries, push them! Find out when you work the hardest, how do you know when you've really worked hard? I have friends who say they know they've worked hard because they 'forgot to eat' others friends have said that they get so tired they need naps between revision. Find out what works for you.

Furthermore, take a step back every two weeks and check how much you've accomplished. It's important to be precise and to use a marker to calculate your work rate. For example, I used the number of text book pages I covered per week to track my progress. When you calculate your work rate ask yourself: Am I doing enough to hit my target or complete my layer by the date I've set? If the answer is no, make further use your free time, particularly on evenings and weekends to boost your work rate.

Make new friends (joking)

"...my friends all got similar grades to me"
-Manos

Those around you shape your assumptions. Your mates in particular have a large part-to-play in what you believe to be true. From my research and experience, students gauge how often or how much they need to work by what their mates are doing. Most of us are naturally inclined to go along with the crowd rather than think independently. It's easy to assume that what you are doing is ok because everyone else is doing it.

Friends...

Furthermore, this influence from others can be so subtle that you don't even notice that it's happening. For example, on a number of occasions I heard my mates say "Don't worry! We can always retake next year". This phrase was etched in my mind and I often re-affirmed it to myself as an excuse to procrastinate. This turned into an assumption that didn't budge because I never chose to question it. It was true, I could re-take my exams if they went wrong. However, I should have been thinking about what would happen if I messed up a bunch of exams then I'd have many more exams in the next sitting and have less time to spend on each one. I shouldn't have continued to reaffirm the damaging assumption. Whenever you think you've made a wrong assumption, tackle it early. Write it down, question and consider the consequences of it.

Further evidence of peer influence can be seen by simply observing friend circles. In my college some groups were known for always doing well and some were known as the 'dossers'. It was clear that the 'dossers' were feeding each other wrong assumptions and constantly reaffirming them. As a result they all underperformed together. However, the opposite occurred with those friend circles doing well. They seemed to directly and indirectly push each other forward through healthy competition. In my experience working with like minded people can propel you even further. This became apparent to me during university where I was one of four graduates who achieved first class honours and given Deans List certificates for academic excellence. The other three were my best mates – this was no coincidence. I'm not saying go and make friends with the geekiest group in your year group, but try and encourage your like minded friends to study with you. It helps knowing some-one else out there is going through the same deal as you.

Family...

It's important to also be aware of the influence of your environment. During first year, my assumptions had built gradually over time from years of seeing my parents watch TV for hours after work, mates jumping on MSN Messenger (or Snapchat and Twitter now) as soon as they got home. As a result, I always assumed that everyone else was doing the same thing.

After my AS results I asked my cousin, who got all A's and is now a doctor, about what he did in the evenings and weekends. I was quite shocked. Not surprisingly his parents worked till late and would encourage him to make the most of those hours. If you are a reactive person and no one physically tells you about other people's habits, then you will assume your study cycle and work ethic is fine. Furthermore, you probably won't go asking about others habits until you realise something is wrong i.e. achieving bad grades.

Smart phones...

Question. What contains a bunch of distractions and follows you around everywhere? You guessed it – your smart phone. With all the games, instant messaging and social media apps, becoming addicted to your phone is not difficult. Above all, the instant messaging apps like WhatsApp and Facebook messenger prove to be the top distractions.

This is because smart phones have made us feel uncomfortable when there is information on the phone that we have not seen yet. Let me ask, do you get uncomfortable about having the little red dot or the 'unread' symbol on the top right of your Facebook, Instagram or WhatsApp icons? Or un-watched stories on Snapchat?

If you find it hard not to click on unread posts/messages/tweets or stories, then you're addicted to social information. You're not alone! Addiction to technology is on the rise and there's a reason for this.

What do you think makes more money than movies, game parks and sports combined? Slot machines. How can slot machines make all this money when they are played with such small amounts of money? They are played with coins. How is this possible? Well, your phone is pretty much an advanced version of a slot machine. Every time you check your phone, you're playing the slot machine to see, what going to appear? Every time you pull down or scroll a news feed, you're playing to see what information you're going to get next. Our obsession with technology is not an accident.

Mobile technology development companies have invested billions of pounds into creating apps that keep us hooked. Some are even hiring PHDs specialising in human psychology and addiction. At the time of this writing, Pokemon Go has been downloaded 100 million times and makes over £1 million a day. Seven out of ten users who download the app, return to it the next day and spend on average forty minutes a day playing the game. Now, do you really think it's possible to study with your phone nearby?

With such a sophisticated piece of technology, you are asking too much of your will power. As your concentration fades during study periods, you become more susceptible to procrastination and seeing the blinking light or push notification on your phone is all it takes to break your concentration. Do yourself a favour. Switch your phone off before you start working and hand it to your mum or dad. Out of sight – out of mind. Doing this alone will probably improve your exam marks by 10% minimum!

Don't leave any room for regret...

You do not want to be one of these people who will regret these 2 years for the rest of your life, knowing that you can do better. It is time for you to be serious and look out for yourself. As much as a social life matters, once you leave college, there will be a very small number of people who you will keep in touch with (and most of them will have followed the same sort of direction as you in life). The rest will disappear to become Facebook contacts. Don't let peer pressure take you away from your aims.

Given the points discussed above, try to become an independent thinker. Don't let the influence of others govern your own actions. Let go of all that and let the contents of this book influence your judgment. It's worked for many others, so why shouldn't it work for you?

6 Step 3 – Motivation:

getting to the table and staying on it

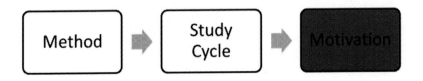

This chapter will show you <u>how</u> to increase your work rate through analysing your day-to-day habits, learning effective motivation techniques and dealing with de-motivating thoughts. After completing this chapter you should be able to fight off procrastination and motivate yourself to study in those free periods, evenings and weekends.

I am aware there is an array of educational and self-help information on this topic. However, we aim to stray away from the ideas that are useless for students and knuckle down into the methods that work.

What is motivation?

Motivation is a word that is thrown around a lot. I believe motivation to be the inner conscious drive that helps you turn a thought or an idea into action. The opposing force to motivation is procrastination. This is the tendency to 'put off' your actions to a later time.

Boosting motivation & destroying procrastination

Motivation and procrastination should be discussed together because they are like Yin & Yang.

When you are highly motivated, you tend to procrastinate less. When you are procrastinating a lot, then it probably means you are low on motivation. All of us have good days (when motivation is high) and bad days when (procrastination is high). I asked several students to describe their good and bad days to see if there were any common characteristics. A lad called Fawaz gave an answer which pretty much encompassed the responses from everyone else. Here's what he said...

Example of a good study day (motivation > procrastination)

"I woke up well rested, feeling quite upbeat and positive. Making a to-do list the night before helped me feel confident about the day ahead. This was because there was some kind of game plan; I felt less uncertain and doubtful. I was still worried about exams but this was keeping me on my toes."

"At college, a guy from the year above told me his success story and it gave me more confidence; if he could do it so could I. This coupled with the positive start made me want to study and I therefore actively looked for moments during the day where I could get started"

"When it finally came to starting, it wasn't a problem and it didn't take long to get momentum on my side. My mind was firmly focused on what I had to do in the present moment and I wasn't dwelling on the past or worrying about the future. It kind of felt like I was on 'autopilot"

"Naturally I became stuck on some questions and got distracted every so often. However, the desire to complete my goals was strong enough to continuously bring me back to the table"

"This momentum continued when I got home from college and I finished the day strong"

Example of a bad study day (procrastination > motivation)

"I had been quite productive over the past few days so woke up feeling good but slightly complacent. Over the course of the day this complacency turned into over confidence and I wasn't really thinking about studying even when the chance presented itself"

"Eventually, when I got home, I decided to sit at my desk and continue from yesterday. I looked through the list of things needed to be done and felt quite overwhelmed. For some reason this got me into a bad mood and therefore, I had trouble concentrating."

"Nevertheless I continued... that's until I got stuck on a practice question. This just added to my frustration. It was a relatively simple question. I lost my confidence and felt insecure about the exam. If I can't do this how am I supposed to do all the other harder questions and get an A?"

"The negative thoughts started snow balling. What if I don't match my offer and don't get into uni? How embarrassing will it be telling my family and friends if I get poor grades? If I don't pull this off will it ruin everything? I then decided to go and eat some food."

"Two hours had passed and I was still reading over the same page of the text book. After convincing myself that I wasn't in the mood to work, I left to watch TV and didn't return for the rest of the evening."

Good days > bad days = higher grades

What Fawaz described above was his typical 'good day' and 'bad day'. It's important to remember that A-Levels are a marathon not a sprint. Therefore the **people who have more good days and less bad days will probably get better grades – it is simple as that!** Before finding out how to boost your good days, I'd like you to follow what Fawaz did; think of any recent good/bad days and make a list of their key characteristics. Fawaz made his own list as shown below:

Characteristics of a Good Day
Positive
Confident – Game plan in place
Feel exam pressure
Heard a success story – it's not impossible
Auto Pilot – Being in the present
Set theme for the day – Set goals early
Un-phased by setback and getting stuck

Characteristics of a Bad Day
Complacent
Over Confident
Overwhelmed – suddenly realising a lot to do.
Frustrated
Insecure - Negative Thoughts
Easily put off by setbacks

Making this list will help you understand your own habits. As you mull over your bad days you will probably realise that they are caused by similar triggers. You may also think of days where you started off well but it all changed when something unexpected

110

happened. When this happens, always try your best to finish the day strong regardless of the setbacks you've experienced during your bad day.

Hopefully now you have an idea of the habits and thoughts which shape how your day goes.

How to increase good study days

In step two of the three step plan we established what the study cycle was and split it into three elements: Intent, Action and Maintenance. Here's a reminder...

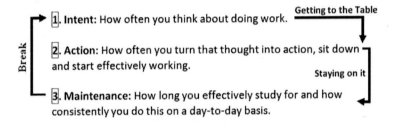

Given that we have determined <u>what</u> these elements are, we are ready to learn <u>how</u> we can be effective in executing each of them. The methods described below will be focusing on improving one or more of each element shown above. Let's start with discussing the most important technique in my opinion – goal setting.

Goal Setting (The Proper Way)

Target study cycle elements - 1 2 3

Goal setting is a way to define exactly what you want to motivate yourself to do. This is a powerful process for thinking about your ideal future, and for motivating yourself to turn this into reality. I'm going to provide a new perspective on effective goal setting. Let's first get the 4 main rules out of the way...

4 golden rules

Each goal should be...

1. Written down

It's important to note that your mind can easily twist, bend and extend goals as time goes by. Writing something down affirms it and makes it tangible. Therefore, to change that goal would mean physically crossing it out or throwing it in the bin. Not the most comfortable thing to do!

If you wake up to read 'I will get 3 As in my A-Levels' every morning, you are more likely to try to feel bad when you sacrifice studying for TV or a night out.

2. Black and white

The goal should be so clear that you know immediately whether you have successfully accomplished it. A pass or fail statement such as "Complete 25 differentiation questions in C2 text book – by 15:00" is much more defined than "Work on differentiation questions for rest of the day." Keep them black and white.

3. Made with a plan and deadline

"A dream is just a dream. A goal is a dream with a plan and a deadline"

Having a plan and deadline will provide structure to the goal. Furthermore, a good game plan will reduce self doubt and feeling insecure about being able to complete what you need on time. Remember back to Fawaz's description of his good day; he mentioned that knowing the game plan helped him feel confident and ultimately played a part in having a 'good day'. Having a plan also helps show that it is achievable and will reduce your doubts.

4. Realistic

There is no point setting yourself unrealistic goals because you will constantly under achieve and lack confidence in your ability. The goal should be ambitious but within reach so that you are able to follow it through and gain confidence from completing it.

Try and stick to these rules so you can get the most out of your goals. Now let's talk about setting goals across time frames...

Goal time frames

Goal setting across multiple time frames will help improve all three elements of your Study Cycle...

Time Frame	Time Span	Example
Long	Years	"I will achieve 3As in my A levels by this time next year"
Medium	Weeks/Days	"Complete 1st rep of chapters 2 & 3 by two weeks from today"
Short	Hours	"Practice questions 1 to 5 – by 14:00"

Long-term goals

These should be set before the start of each academic year and never change. Even now, after university and starting my business, all the long-term goals I've ever made are printed out and still stuck on my wall...

"I will achieve 3A's in my A-Levels by June 2006" **√**

113

"I will achieve a 1st Class Honors in my Degree by June 2009" ✔

"I will be accepted on to an Internship Program at an Investment Bank by June 2009" ✔

"I will write a book to show A-Level students how to improve their grades by December 2013" ✔

"I will write a book to show GCSE students how to improve their grades by March 2015" ✔

"I will write a book to show university students how to succeed by October 2017"

Every time a goal was achieved I would draw a large tick on the page and every time a goal expired without me achieving it, I either extended it or wrote a new one. I recommend doing the same: write or print your long-term goals out in large, bold font on A4 paper. Then stick them up right in front of your desk.

Finally, give yourself a small print or a disclaimer on those goals to help keep the goal fresh; somewhat like the following:

"I know this goal will try and fade away over time but I must try and fight to keep it close"

Ace Tips

It is all well and good writing what you want on a piece of paper. However, to really be effective you have to work hard inside your mind. You must really want to do well and achieve the goals you set.

One university student I was mentoring explained, at the start of the academic year, that he wanted to achieve a First Class Honors in his degree. He took my advice and wrote this goal down and pinned it up in his work area. At the end of his academic year and after his last exam I asked him how he got on and he replied "Ye OK...should have passed." This clearly showed that at some point during the year his goal changed from 70% (First Class) to 40% (A Pass). A person who really wanted a First would have been kicking and screaming over the possibility of not achieving what he/she set out to do.

Medium-term goals

Goals across weeks and days will help you piece together the long-term plan. Set the goals to give you some room to manoeuvre in case it takes longer than expected. Once these goals are set you can gauge whether you are working hard enough to complete layers in time for the exam and adjust your time accordingly.

Earlier our student Fawaz mentioned that a bad day can be caused by feeling overwhelmed by the amount of work needed to be completed. Having medium-term goals on paper will help attenuate these feelings because it will show a realistic and achievable plan.

As a final note, when setting goals for the day it is best to get your least favourite pieces of work out of the way first when you're fresh and motivation is high. It will help you build momentum and continue on with the rest of the days goals.

<u>Accountability</u>

For goals in any time frame, sharing them with your parents or friends makes you accountable for getting them done. This is an effective way of motivating yourself to achieve what you set out to do. This uses our inherent nature to compete and feel better than others and can be demonstrated by my treadmill analogy...

When you go to the gym and jump on a treadmill next to somebody, you immediately feel the need to run faster and longer than them. Even if they are a stranger! The feeling is magnified when you go for a run with a friend or someone you know. The same can be applied to academic study. However, because studying is an individual task, you have to create the competition yourself!

This can be done using a weekly e-mail. For example, every Monday you and a friend can send each other's performance for the week ahead and evaluate the week at the end. Even though most of the time you know your mates won't say anything or judge you if you are slacking, a natural competitive tendency will encourage you to be better than them. The mere thought of someone else knowing your underachievement and even the act of lying about it will be uncomfortable. Furthermore, if you haven't completed any of your goals at the end of the week, you'll feel a bit pants and should hopefully try to push yourself further the next week.

Short-term goals – the goal achieving junky

Target study cycle elements - 3

Here we are going to talk about how to 'stay in the present moment' and focus on the task at hand. The name 'Goal achieving junky', as strange it may sound, is exactly the type of idea I want to promote to you. I want you to open your mind to becoming a short-term results driven addict. Someone who not only makes goals and pushes to achieve them, but also craves the feeling of achieving them again and again.

This isn't really a technique of any sort but more just a change in attitude or habit. Start scribbling down or typing out goals regularly. These can be on – paper, post it notes or your mobile phone.

During our research, we found many students wrote multiple reminders of their short and long-term goals all over the place from their bedroom to their bathroom! It also helps to physically tick or cross them off when they are complete.

This works because you associate 'good behaviour' with a positive result. Just like how you give a dog a treat if he sits when you ask him to! Working hard would be equivalent to 'good behaviour' and hitting the target/crossing it off the page would be the positive stimulus. This will help you achieve three things:

1. Help you work effectively for longer.
2. Encourage you to drive for results and finish tasks through rather than leaving them half way.
3. Provide continuous results that you will feel good about and therefore help keep your mind fully focused on the task at hand.

Remember you have to approach studying like how an athlete would with his physical training or how an Olympian would push themselves by thinking one more rep or one more lap, you have to think one more page or one more goal.

Target study cycle elements - 2 & 3

Although childish, bribing yourself is a useful way of giving that extra push to hit your short time-frame targets. It will also help you to condition yourself into being a more results driven person who looks forward to finishing tasks thoroughly and detests leaving things half way. Additionally, bribes and treats can be incorporated into the goals you set at the start of the day. For example:

1. Last 10 pages of mammalian behaviour chapter
2. 15 min break and sandwich snack
3. First 20 pages of second order differentiation
4. 30 min - Eastenders

It is important to ensure that the treats you choose don't let you get carried away and cause you to waste more time than you accounted for. When you are taking a break it is much easier to say 10 more minutes of TV then it is to say 10 more minutes of biology. Here are my 5 best and worst self bribes:

5 best:
1. Short burst of intensive exercise - 10 min sit ups
2. Short walk or fresh air
3. Small snack
4. Shower
5. Short TV programme

5 worst:
1. Heavy meal
2. Starting a movie
3. Shopping
4. Drinking
5. Games console

Target study cycle elements - 1 & 2

Have you ever had a time where you just can't seem to build any momentum? Every time you attempt to work, it all goes square and nothing gets done? Me too.

The damage comes when the 'slow patch' continues and then becomes the norm or a habit. Therefore, it's important to be aware of when it happens and to take action. Taking action can sometimes be hard, but, with three simple steps, you should be able to get over the hill.

> **Step one:** Recognise whether something is a one off or if it is turning into a spiralling habit.

> **Step two:** Have the discipline to make a personal change to break that habit. The longer you leave it running the harder it will be to break.

> **Step three:** Take action by doing something out of your comfort zone, i.e. something you would not normally do.

I remember after successfully completing my January AS retakes (back when January exams existed) I decided to take a break for 2 weeks. Following a few nights out, I attempted to build momentum and get back into the routine. I was too complacent and it just wasn't happening. This continued for another 2 weeks until a friend helped me realise that continuing in this way will undo all my hard work in the first term. I'm glad I took the break I deserved and needed it, but I had to find a way to get back into routine...

As an arguable 'punishment' for myself I took my books, told my girlfriend to leave me alone for a couple of days, got my mum to take my phone, drop me to my grandma's house and just leave me there for a few days. Looking back makes me both cringe and chuckle. My grandma was a very spiritual lady who meditated for hours on end. I hoped that by staying there I could soak up some of that spirituality and it would somehow help me break out of my cycle. It felt like I was going on my very own A-Level spiritual retreat and guess what? It worked! While I didn't turn into a meditating 18 year old, over those few days I worked efficiently, hit all my goals and got right back on track.

Back then I was kind of spooked and thought perhaps the spirituality actually helped me change course. In hindsight, it was the random shift in environment, boredom (no TV) and early starts because my grandma woke me up with her bell ringing/chanting. Regardless, these factors caused enough of a high impact to change my destructive habit and get right back on course.

Motivational springboard

Target study cycle elements - 3

Have you ever been really motivated by an inspiring person before? I'm sure you have. Their ideas, opinions, charisma and inspirational language can provide a real motivation boost especially if you're having a 'bad day'. It's unfortunate we can't experience that 'umph!' all the time because we naturally have low periods every now and again. Well you can't read a motivational piece of text every time you feel less motivated right? Well, why not!? There are hundreds of books, websites, YouTube videos, Facebook pages, celebrity biographies etc which you can use to give a quick boost when feeling de-motivated. Use these as a spring board to get yourself out of a period of low motivation. Beware, don't use this as an excuse to procrastinate!

Target study cycle elements - 2

This is a weird albeit effective technique for when you are close to hitting your target but running low on concentration. To grab those last few minutes of your attention span, use your mind to narrate the information in your text book using someone else's voice. This could be anyone's voice but personally I like using David Attenborough! I find his voice quite distinctive and it makes me want to listen to what he's saying. Have a go – no harm in trying!

Ejection seat (coming close to something then bailing at the last moment)

Target study cycle elements - 2

This little trick can help you avoid procrastination. It should be used when you know you need to start working and there is something you are really tempted to do such as watch TV, read a magazine, or play a video game. Bring yourself really close to doing it then bail at the last minute – like how a fighter pilot ejects before crashing. The more emphatically you do this the better! For example, if you want to watch TV, then go towards the remote, pick it up, point it at the TV but then suddenly and emphatically chuck on to the sofa. Then turn around immediately and go to your desk!

Dealing with the devil on your shoulder... de-motivating thoughts

Our minds are complex things that scientists still know very little about. All we know is that our actions are influenced by our thoughts and emotions. Controlling our emotions to benefit us is a skill that some do better than others. However, through understanding and practice it's possible to develop the attributes you require to bring order to the chaos.

Earlier we saw how Fawaz spiralled from being confident, to insecure, after falling into a bad mood and experiencing a setback. He stopped thinking about the present moment and started worrying about the future. Eventually this made him unproductive, feel too overwhelmed and he gave up. We can never completely avoid bad days like this but we can limit them simply by monitoring and understanding our de-motivating thoughts. The key is to remember is that these thoughts are emotional and are caused by irrationality.

In our research three core issues continuously popped up: lack of self belief, fear of failure and inability to see immediate results. In this section I will outline the best solutions to tackle them.

Lack of self belief –"I'm not good enough to..."

You hear parents and coaches tell their kids in Hollywood sports movies all the time "Believe in yourself son". What does this mean? Let's break it down.

Self belief is trust in your ability to accomplish what you set out to do. If you lack self belief you've essentially convinced yourself the decision that it is unattainable.

Why do people have low self-belief?

People have low self-belief because they are insecure about their intelligence, quality of school, past results, low attention span and self-motivation. Most of the time these insecurities are exaggerated and have to be kept at bay in order for success. Everyone is insecure on some level because our minds are wired in that way. A little insecurity can keep you on your toes but, a lot of it can hold you back from achieving what you want.

I know this because I hit the lowest low after seeing my AS results. On the surface, I blamed everything. For example I blamed my teachers; however, deep down I blamed my own attributes. I was convinced that my poor grades were mostly down to the low intelligence that I inherited from my parents. At one point I even suggested that I had some sort of attention-deficit disorder. Eventually, I realised how irrational these thoughts were, but it wasn't enough to keep them at bay.

I would have short moments where I believed in my ability, but then long periods where I would think 'Who am I kidding? What are the chances of actually pulling this off?' This was evidence that I didn't truly believe I could get the grades I wanted. If I stood any chance of turning this situation around, I had to come up with some solution.

Solution:

Firstly, keep an open mind when it comes to your own ability; just remember many others have experienced the same lack of self belief. On their own, they came to realise how irrational it was and still succeeded.

Secondly, if you have hit rock bottom then I want you to embrace that and let yourself be bitter about being there. Feel 'comfortably pissed off' by the situation and understand from this point onwards you have absolutely nothing to lose. Snarl at your AS or predicted grades and have the audacity to challenge yourself to achieve straight A's. Say to yourself, I want a full set of A's and I'm going to get them at all costs. Dismiss any thought of damage control suggesting you should try and salvage some B's and C's. Finally, affirm the following:

'Life is too short to just sit and accept my short comings. I'm going to attempt the so called 'impossible'. I'm going to throw everything I have at these exams. If I don't get what I want, only then will I accept that I am not cut out for this. These commitments I'm making will try to fade over time but I must fight to keep them close'

The affirmation above was the reaction I had after receiving my AS results. It enabled me to experience that quite sudden paradigm shift where I turned into a highly effective person. You can do the same if you execute the suggestions in this book.

Fear - "what if..."

The emotion of fear exists to help us steer clear of unfavourable experiences. Our minds constantly run through different scenarios that we are fearful of, which is why we constantly ask ourselves "What if...".

When you're afraid, even if you've decided to take on a challenge, a part of you is determined to avoid going forward. This slows you down and makes you careful, which is useful. However, sometimes your fears are based on your imagination rather than an accurate assessment of the risks in your reality.

Even if you have a strong desire to move forward, the 'safety' emotion of fear will kick in, and prevent you from pursuing something of benefit to you.

For students we found the most common fear was:

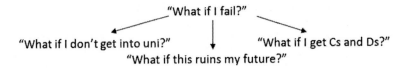

"What if I fail?"

"What if I don't get into uni?"   "What if I get Cs and Ds?"

"What if this ruins my future?"

Such fears will keep you on your toes and help improve all three elements of your study cycle.

The destructive fear factor

In many cases fear can be such a strong emotion that it becomes demoralising; especially if you've tasted failure before and are worried that it may happen again. If untreated this can manifest into a destructive emotion and de-motivate you because it's such a bitter pill to swallow if you don't succeed. In our research, 76% of students mentioned that a fear of failure hindered their performance instead of helping.

Solution:

Ideally, every time we have an aggressive fear, we should follow the flow chart below...

Fear Flow Chart

```
                         ┌──────────┐
        ┌────────────────┤   Fear   ├────────────────┐
        │                └──────────┘                │
        ▼                   No                        ▼
┌───────────────────┐ ────────────────►  ┌───────────────────┐
│ Is it a fear of   │                    │ Is it a fear of   │
│ the past          │◄──────────────     │ the future?       │
│ repeating itself? │      No            │                   │
└───────────────────┘                    └───────────────────┘
        │ Yes                                    │ Yes
        ▼                                        ▼
┌───────────────────┐              ┌───────────────────┐
│  Past ≠ Future    │         No   │ Do you have       │
│                   │              │ control over      │
└───────────────────┘              │ the outcome?      │
        │                          └───────────────────┘
        ▼                                  │ Yes
┌───────────────────┐              ┌───────────────────┐
│   Don't worry!    │◄─────────────│                   │
│                   │              │        X          │
└───────────────────┘              └───────────────────┘
```

Obviously, this is easier said than done!

That 'X' in the flow chart isn't an error. It's just to represent the only variable in the flow chart. Before talking about variable 'X' let's talk about the two things we cannot change i.e. the constants...

1. Fearing the past will repeat itself - There is no such thing as a run of bad luck. People believe in nonsense like this because the human brain creates patterns out of random events, discards contradicting evidence and remembers the events that fit the pattern. Unfortunately for most of us, the hurt of losing is more memorable than the euphoria of winning. You have to flip this on its head. Try adopting a short-term memory when it comes to bad experiences from the past and a long-term memory for your successes.

126

2. Worrying over, or being scared of a future scenario that you <u>cannot control is a waste of time</u> because there is no way to predict the future. Understand that the way it plays out in your mind is only imagination and is far from reality. Keep reminding yourself of this fact.

You have all the tools, so let's talk about variable 'X'...

If you have debilitating fears of certain scenarios or outcomes occurring in the future, that you <u>can control</u>, (like you're revision) then there are steps you can take to help. Firstly, the best way is to have an effective plan in place that you believe in. If you understand and execute the methods discussed in this book, particularly within the '3 steps', you will begin to see your fears fade. The methods in 'Step 1' will help you absorb information more effectively; noticing your work ethic improve will naturally shift your sight from fear of failure to euphoria of success. This is exactly what I experienced.

During first year, I was constantly in fear. What if I don't finish my revision on time? What if I run out of time in the exam? What if I go in and I forget everything?

When I got my act together in second year, these fears were still lingering around but it was easy to push them aside. This was because I believed my plan would work and while executing it I could see evidence it was working. When it finally came to exams, I knew that I'd given myself the best possible chance to succeed and there wasn't much more I could do. I then entered the exam hall confident and, most importantly, fearless.

Remember - there have been many others in your position, who have felt the same demoralising fear and conquered it to significantly improve their grades.

As a final note, by succumbing to our fears, we end up cordoning off large areas of our own ability. Life is inescapably risky and painful, not to mention 100% fatal. So don't feel you can dodge a bit of pain by backing down from something a bit scary. Face your fears and go for it!

Inability to see immediate results

Most things worth achieving usually take a lot of time and effort. A-Levels are no different. For both A-Level years there are approximately 9 months from the point you receive your syllabus to the point of your exams. Then the whole summer to get through before results. Near the end of my second AS level term, I had around 6 weeks left till the summer exams. I vividly remember feeling like exams were still so far away. I didn't really address the possibility that I'd leave it too late and was coasting through the year thinking everything will kind of sort itself out; the familiar phrase of 'I'll start working hard soon' continuously popped up. Of course soon came too late and not enough layers were completed in time.

Near the beginning of these 6 weeks, I remember attempting to sit at the table to revise for a physics exam. The script and conversation in my head went more or less like this:

'oh look its 7:30pm maybe I should go over some physics'

I sit down at the table and stare at my text book and 5 minutes later...

'This is pretty hard, maybe I'll watch TV for a bit – there are still a few weeks left so what is half an hour going to change anyway? I'll concentrate after'

I go watch TV and half an hour turns into an hour, an hour turns into 2 hours and low and behold I never return till the next evening when the same thing happens again.

The complacency of knowing there was ample time before an exam prevented me from actually getting started and hitting my stride. At the time I thought half an hour here or there would contribute very little to achieving my final grade. This was probably true if it was just a one off. However, because I let myself get away with it so many times, it became a bad habit. Now the problem was that hours of time were lost and this cycle could have been corrected by a proactive approach to the issue.

Solution:

It dawned on me then that being an effective person is all about how you condition yourself. It's about proactively producing that deadline pressure on your own, not reacting late to external forces and understanding that you need to make a sacrifice now for what you want eventually.

The most fundamental way of making this happen is by setting your own deadlines in advance of those that are given to you. As I mentioned in chapter 4, after making my proactive plan at the start of second year college, I finished the first layer for some of my exams before my teachers got round to teaching them. In fact I used the classroom lessons as a 2nd layer and not so surprisingly these were the modules I hit the highest grades in.

In addition to setting your own deadlines, if you find yourself constantly justifying your procrastination by the amount of time there is then it is important to focus on the process rather than the result. This can be explained by the wall analogy:

"You don't set out to build a wall. You don't say 'I'm going to build the biggest, baddest, greatest wall that's ever been built.' You don't start there. You say, 'I'm going to lay this brick as perfectly as a brick can be laid. You do that every single day. And soon you have a wall."
-- Will Smith

Think of yourself as an athlete. The individual who stays down on the table, absorbs the most information and does the most layers will get the better grade; just how a footy team that wins the most and loses the least number of matches wins the league. Each day should be seen as an important match. You will have some missed matches, surprise defeats and some draws but overall if you keep winning the result will present itself at the end.

When it comes to forgetting the result and concentrating on the process there is no better advice than to be a short-term goal setting junky. Keep jotting down goals and deadlines. This way you can create your own little victories throughout each day and become immersed in the process.

Onwards & upwards...

7 Gap year or no gap year?

You may decide to take a gap year. Make the most of this. Volunteer, travel or work. Use it wisely, for it is a year many would love to take. A lot of people are sceptical about taking a gap year, so here are some of the advantages and disadvantages of taking the plunge:

Advantages

1. It's a unique opportunity and allows you to take a break. You will rarely get the opportunity to take so much time out without having anything else to worry about.

2. The gap year can help you find out more about yourself, your interests and hobbies. At the end of it, you may find you know what you want to do for the rest of your life. You may find out more about your strengths and weaknesses and knowing this will make you a stronger person. This will probably raise your confidence at future interviews.

3. It is a chance to show yourself off to future employers. Many employers will be interested in what you did in your gap year. Often, it is important to them that they find some-one who is a well rounded person and has interests/hobbies outside of work.

4. It can improve your performance at university. There has been some anecdotal evidence from students in America published by the 'American Gap Association' that shows

133

that students benefit significantly from taking time off. A study by the dean of admissions at Middlebury College found that the average grades for Middlebury students who had taken a gap year were consistently higher than those who had not.

During university many of my friends and I applied for summer internships and graduate positions. I found that those who completed gap year placements at companies were receiving interviews and offers left right and centre. This was because they had experienced high pressured interviews before and had adopted the correct professional attitude required to impress graduate employers. Also the placements helped them develop important communication, team work and leadership skills.

If used properly, a gap year can be both extremely rewarding and exciting.

Disadvantages

1) The major disadvantage of taking a gap year is that **it can be possible to waste the year.** It's very easy to make elaborate plans for a gap year, and instead do nothing and spend 6 months watching TV. This is what you don't want. Employers will not look kindly to this, and they will ask you how you spent your year. It will reflect badly on you, no matter what excuses you can provide. Therefore, it is essential that if you are to take a gap year, you plan well and ensure that you complete what you set out to do.

What you can do in your gap year

The most important thing to remember, when planning your gap year, is that it is an extremely personal year. It is a year about you. This year is something that is going to be a talking point for a lot of important people that you meet in the future, including your potential managers, colleagues, new friends and even your in-laws. Use this year to home in on what interests and inspires you.

Although having fun is absolutely one of the most important aspects a successful gap year, you must also consider the equally important factor of... How will this gap year help me in the future? Successful gap years usually combine the following two criteria:

1) To gain experience in a specific career/job (through direct work experience or internship).

2) Volunteer work

Both of these types of gap years are looked upon extremely highly amongst future employers, and look great on your CV. To have a successful gap year, you should try to have two of the above criteria.

Volunteer work abroad
If you know what you want to do for the rest of your life, and if it is a competitive field, it is important that you ensure that part of your gap year is spent gaining experience within this sector. If you do not however know what career path you want to pursue, you should spend at least part of the gap year trying to gain some experience and focus on potential career paths which interest you. The best thing about gap years is that, as long as you are following the above criteria, what you actually do or where you do it is entirely up to what inspires you and what you feel will give you the greatest amount of enjoyment! You can make it as varied as you like.

For example, you could choose to do a fashion internship in New York the first part of your gap year, and the second living with local people saving turtles in northern Africa!

8 <u>Life after A-Levels</u>

After your A-Levels are over, you will be ready to start a new and exciting time in your life. University life, freshers, new friends, new course, new accommodation, a new student bank account and some new clothes; you'll be all set to embark on the most enjoyable few years of your life.

It will be a time when you say farewell to your old friends. The closest of you will keep in touch. Many will become Facebook friends. In five years you will be shocked to see how much people have changed in both appearance and attitude. A few, however, won't change at all.

Many of you will go off on your own to university and be very career focused. While some of you will decide university isn't for you, either for financial reasons or wanting to do vocational qualifications. Your time in school was not a waste - you picked up valuable skills and you will have left school with top A-Level grades, putting you at an advantage above other school levers like yourself.

Some of you will not receive the grades required to get into the university you desire. You may decide to spend the year retaking, go travelling, or to choose a course in clearing. For those of you who choose the latter, I would ask you to think about this carefully. Are you willing to study this course just because you want the university experience and don't 'waste' a year, or do you actually want to study the course? Going to university is fun, but expensive, so it's important to consider all your options. It is only then that you truly learn the skills and abilities that university is designed to teach you.

Whichever path you choose, if you ever have to take exams in the future, the techniques you learnt from this book will stay with you and can continue to be used to help pass exams for the rest of your life.

We wish you a happy and safe journey as you travel above and beyond your A-Level years. Well done – you've done it!

Appendix 1: Table comparing traditional note taking to the scribble technique.

For arguments sake let's say you have 3 weeks total to learn for a specific exam. The percentages below were calculated through our own research and may not apply to everyone.

		Traditional Note Taking	Scribble Technique
Week 1 - Rep 1	Time	This first repetition will take relatively long because notes have to be both neatly written and accurate. Also, as the material will be new and un-familiar. Rate of learning = 12 sides an hour.	Similar to traditional note taking, fresh and unfamiliar material will impact the time required to complete this repetition. However, reading, closing the book and scribbling will be quite a fast process. Rate of learning = 10 sides an hour.
	Retention	I have now made notes equating to approx. 70% of the total information in the text book. Of this let's say I can retain 30% of my notes so the net retention of the textbook is 21% (30% of 70%). This declines quite rapidly over time.	I've studied in detail through 100% of the total information in the text book. Of this I can retain 40% and the net retention is 40%. This declines relatively slowly over time.
Week 2 -Rep2	Time	Naturally, the 2nd rep is faster because the information is familiar and I'm focusing more on learning than writing neatly. Rate of learning = 15 sides an hour.	Even though a lot of information was covered on the first rep, each page I turn to is familiar. Therefore this rep is much faster. Rate of learning = 15 sides an hour.
	Retention	I'm retaining a lot more. My notes cover 70% of the text book and I am retaining 60% of my notes. Net retention = 42%.	The 2nd layer of information means I'm retaining 20% more information. This means I'm retaining 60% of the text book. Net retention = 60%.

Week 3 - Rep 3	Time	Now I'm just reading over my notes and highlighting/re-writing bits I keep forgetting. Learning rate = 20 sides an hour.	This 3rd rep is much faster. All I'm doing is skimming over the pages and only covering/scribbling parts that are not familiar. Learning rate = 20 sides an hour
	Retention	Covering the material a 3rd time means I now retain 80% of my notes from 70% of the syllabus. Net retention = 56%.	A 3rd layer has boosted my retention up another 10% and I can pretty much remember 70% of the text book. This doesn't mean I can re-write it word for word but most exam questions I could quite easily remember enough points to get full marks. Net retention = 70%.